Merhaba!

Just Enough **Turkish**

D. L. Ellis

Roderick Conway Morris

New York   Chicago   San Francisco   Lisbon   London   Madrid   Mexico City
Milan   New Delhi   San Juan   Seoul   Singapore   Sydney   Toronto

The McGraw·Hill Companies

Library of Congress Cataloging-in-Publication Data

Ellis, D. L.
      Just enough Turkish / D.L. Ellis, Roderick Conway Morris.
          p.   cm.
      Includes bibliographical references and index.
      ISBN 0-8442-9518-3
      1. Turkish language—Conversation and phrase books—English.
I. Morris, Roderick Conway.   II. Title.

PL127.E46   2006
494'3583421—dc22   2006043213

14 15 16 17 18 19 20 21 22 23   QFR/QFR   1 5 4 3 2

ISBN 978-0-8442-9518-3
MHID   0-8442-9518-3

McGraw-Hill books are available at special quantity discounts to use as premiums and sales promotions or for use in corporate training programs. To contact a representative, please visit the Contact Us pages at www.mhprofessional.com.

Roderick Conway Morris would like to thank Professor Süheyla Artemel of Boğaziçi University, Istanbul, for her generous help and advice, and Dr. Antony Greenwood and the American Research Institute in Turkey for their assistance and hospitality.

The publishers are also grateful to the Turkish Tourist and Information Office for their help in the preparation of this book.

This book is printed on acid-free paper.

Contents

Using this phrase book

- This phrase book is designed to help you get by in Turkey, to get what you want or need. It concentrates on the simplest but most effective way you can express these needs in an unfamiliar language.
- The **Contents** on p. 5 give you a good idea of which section to consult for the phrase you need.
- The **Index** on p. 142 gives you more detailed information about where to look for your phrase.
- When you have found the right page you will be given:
  either – the exact phrase
  or   – help in making up a suitable sentence
  and – help in getting the pronunciation right.
- The English sentences in **bold type** will be useful for you in a variety of different situations, so they are worth learning by heart. (See also **Do it yourself**, p. 135.)
- Wherever possible you will find help in understanding what Turkish people say to you in reply to your questions.
- If you want to practise the basic nuts and bolts of the language further, look at the **Do it yourself** section starting on p. 135.
- Note especially these three sections:
  Everyday expressions, p. 10
  Shop talk, p. 50
  Sign Language, p. 114.
  You are sure to want to refer to them most frequently.
- Once abroad, remember to make good use of the local tourist offices (see p. 22).

North American address:
The Turkish Tourism Office
1714 Massachusetts Avenue NW
Washington, DC 20036
Tel.: (202) 429-9844

A note on the pronunciation system

Turkish is not a difficult language for English speakers to pronounce, and the Turkish alphabet, although containing a few unfamiliar variations of letters, is almost identical to our own. So to make things easier and to help make the phrase book instantly usable without any preparation, below each sentence the words are written out in a simplified form. This system is not phonetical, but if you follow it what you say should be readily comprehensible to Turkish speakers. One thing to remember is to lay the stress on the syllables in italics, e.g. **iyi akşamlar** (ee-*yee* ahk-shahm-l*ahr*): 'good evening/night'.

In fact the stress on words in Turkish tends to be more even than in English, with the emphasis usually falling on the last syllable of the word (although with place names it often falls on the first or second syllable). However, even if your pronunciation is not quite right you will generally find that you are understood, since most Turks are good and willing listeners and are genuinely pleased when foreigners take the trouble to try to speak Turkish.

Letter	Pronunciation	Letter	Pronunciation
A a	**a** as in father	L l	**l** as in long
Â â	**aa** as in baa	M m	**m** as in mother
B b	**b** as in but	N n	**n** as in no
C c	**j** as in judge	O o	**o** as in opera
Ç ç	**ch** as in chat	Ö ö	like **ea** in early
D d	**d** as in dot		
E e	**e** as in bed	P p	**p** as in pot
F f	**f** as in four	R r	**r** as in red
G g	**g** as in good	S s	**s** as in some
Ğ ğ	not pronounced, but makes the letter before slightly longer	Ş ş	**sh** as in shop
		T t	**t** as in tell
		U u	**u** as in put
H h	**h** as in have	Ü ü	as the Scots say the **u** in put
İ i	**i** as in sit		
I ı	**i** as in Cyril	V v	**v** as in very
J j	like **s** in pleasure	Y y	**y** as in yet
		Z z	**z** as in zero
K k	**k** as in kite		

Kolay gelsin! Roderick Conway Morris

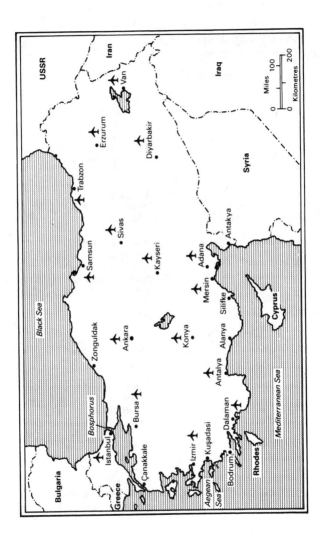

Everyday expressions

[See also 'Shop talk', p. 50]

Hello	**Merhaba** mehr-hah-bah
Good morning	**Günaydın** gooh-nay-duhn
Good afternoon	**İyi günler** ee-yee goohn-lehr
Good evening	**İyi akşamlar** ee-yee ahk-shahm-lahr
Good night	**İyi geceler** ee-yee gheh-jeh-lehr
Goodbye [person staying]	**Güle güle** gooh-leh gooh-leh
Goodbye [person leaving]	**Allahaısmarladık** ahl-lahs-mahr-lah-duhk
See you later	**Tekrar görüşürüz** tehk-rahr gher-rooh-shooh-roohz
Yes	**Evet** eh-vet
Please	**Lütfen** looht-fehn
Yes, please	**Evet lütfen** eh-vet, looht-fehn
Great!	**Güzel!** gooh-zehl
Thank you	**Teşekkür ederim** Teh-shehk-koohr eh-deh-reem
Thank you very much	**Çok teşekkür ederim** chohk teh-shehk-koohr eh-deh-reem
That's right	**Doğru** doh-roo
No	**Hayır** hah-yuhr
No, thank you	**Hayır, teşekkür ederim** hah-yuhr teh-shehk-koohr eh-deh-reem

I disagree	**Öyle değil** er-leh deh-*eel*
Excuse me ⎤ Sorry ⎦	**Affedersiniz** ahf-feh-dehr-see-n*ee*z
Don't mention it ⎤ That's OK ⎦	**Bir şey değil** beer shehy dee-*eel*
That's good ⎤ I like it ⎦	**Tamam** tah-m*ah*m
That's no good ⎤ I don't like it ⎦	**Tamam değil** tah-m*ah*m dee-*eel*
I know	**Biliyorum** bee-*lee*-yoh-room
I don't know	**Bilmiyorum** b*eel*-mee-yoh-room
It doesn't matter	**Zararı yok** zah-rah-r*uh* yohk
Where's the toilet, please?	**Tuvalet nerede, lütfen?** too-wah-l*eh*t neh-reh-d*eh* l*oo*ht-fehn
How much is that? [*point*]	**Bu ne kadar?** boo neh kah-d*ah*r
Is the service included?	**Servis dahil mi?** sehr-v*ee*s dah-h*ee*l mee
Do you speak English?	**İngilizce biliyor musunuz?** Een-ghee-l*ee*z-jeh bee-*lee*-yohr moo-soo-n*oo*z
I'm sorry . . .	**Özür dilerim . . .** er-z*oo*hr dee-leh-r*ee*m
I don't speak Turkish	**Türkçe bilmiyorum** t*oo*hrk-cheh b*eel*-mee-yoh-room
I only speak a little Turkish	**Pek az Türkçe biliyorum** pehk ahz t*oo*hrk-cheh bee-*lee*-yoh-room
I don't understand	**Anlamıyorum** ahn-l*ah*-muh-yoh-room
Please can you . . .	**Lütfen . . .** l*oo*ht-fehn
repeat that	**tekrarlayınız** tehk-rahr-lah-yuh-n*uh*z
speak more slowly	**daha yavaş konuşunuz** dah-h*ah* yah-v*ah*sh koh-noo-shoo-n*oo*z

write it down **yazınız**
yah-zuh-n*u*hz

What is this called in Turkish? **Türkçe bunun adı ne?**
[*point*] t*oo*hrk-cheh boo-n*oo*n ah-d*u*h
neh

Crossing the border

ESSENTIAL INFORMATION

- Don't waste time before you leave rehearsing what you're going to say to the border officials – the chances are that you won't have to say anything at all, especially if you travel by air.
- It is more useful to check that you have your documents handy for the journey: passport, tickets, money, travellers' cheques, insurance documents, driving licence and car registration documents.
- Look our for these signs:
  SINIR (border)
  DUR (stop)
  PASAPORT KONTROLU (passport control)
  GÜMRÜK (customs)
  KAMBİYO (exchange)
  VARIŞ (arrival)
  ÇIKIŞ (departure)
  [*For further signs and notices, see p. 114*]
- You may be asked routine questions by the customs officials [*see below*]. If you have to give personal details, see 'Meeting people', p. 13. The other important answer to know is 'Nothing': **Hiç** (heech).

ROUTINE QUESTIONS

Passport? **Pasaport?**
pah-sah-p*o*hrt

Insurance? **Sigorta?**
see-g*o*hr-tah

Driving licence?	**Şoför ehliyeti** shoh-fer eh-lee-yeh-*tee*
Green card	**Yeşil kart** yeh-sheel kahrt
Ticket, please	**Bilet, lütfen** bee-leht looht-fehn
Have you anything to declare?	**Deklare edecek bir şeyiniz var mı?** deh-klah-reh eh-deh-jehk beer sheh-yee-neez vahr muh
Where are you going?	**Nereye gidiyorsunuz?** neh-reh-yeh ghee-dee-yohr-soo- nooz
How long are you staying?	**Ne kadar kalacaksınız?** neh kah-dahr kah-lah-jahk-suh- nuhz
Where have you come from?	**Nereden geldiniz?** neh-reh-dehn ghehl-dee-neez

You may also have to fill in forms which ask for:

surname	**soyadı**
first name	**adı**
date of birth	**doğum tarihi**
address	**adres**
nationality	**uyruk**
profession	**meslek**
passport number	**pasaport numarası**
issued at	**verildiği yer**
place of birth	**doğum yeri**
signature	**imza**

Meeting people

[*See also 'Everyday expressions', p. 10*]

Breaking the ice

Hello	**Merhaba** mehr-hah-bah

Good day	**İyi günler**
	ee-yee goohn-lehr
How are you?	**Nasılsınız?**
	nah-suhl-suh-nuhz
I am well	**İyiyim**
	ee-yee-yeem
And you?	**Ya siz?**
	yah seez
Pleased to meet you	**Memnun oldum**
	mehm-noon ohl-doom
I am here . . .	**Buradayım . . .**
	boo-rah-dah-yuhm
on holiday	**tatil için**
	tah-teel ee-cheen
on business	**iş için**
	eesh ee-cheen
Would you like . . .	**. . . ister misiniz?**
	ees-tehr mee-see-neez
a drink?	**Bir içki**
	beer eech-kee
a cigarette?	**Bir sigara**
	beer see-gah-rah
a cigar?	**Bir puro**
	beer poo-roh

Name

What's your name?	**Adınız ne?**
	ah-duh-nuhz neh
My name is . . .	**Adım . . .**
	ah-duhm

Family

Are you married?	**Evli misiniz?**
	ehv-lee mee-see-neez
I am married	**Evliyim**
	ehv-lee-yeem
I am single	**Bekârım**
	beh-kyah-ruhm
This is . . .	**Bu . . .**
	boo

my wife	**eşim**
	eh-sh*ee*m
my husband	**eşim**
	eh-sh*ee*m
my son	**oğlum**
	oh-l*oo*m
my daughter	**kızım**
	kuh-z*u*hm
my friend	**arkadaşım**
	ahr-kah-dah-sh*u*hm
my colleague	**meslektaşım**
	mehs-lehk-tah-sh*u*hm
Do you have any children?	**Çocuğunuz var mı?**
	choh-joo-oo-n*oo*z vahr muh
I have . . .	**. . . var**
	vahr
one daughter	**Bir kızım**
	beer kuh-z*u*hm
one son	**Bir oğlum**
	beer oh-l*oo*m
two daughters	**İki kızım**
	ee-k*ee* kuh-z*u*hm
three sons	**Üç oğlum . . .**
	oohch oh-l*oo*m
No, I haven't any children	**Hayır, çocuğum yok**
	h*a*h-yuhr choh-joo-*oo*m yohk

Where you live

Are you Turkish?	**Türk müsünüz?**
	toohrk mooh-sooh-n*oo*hz
I am English	**İngilizim**
	een-ghee-leez-*ee*m
I am American	**Amerikalıyım**
	ah-meh-ree-kah-luh-y*u*hm

[*For other nationalities, see p. 128*]

Where are you from?

I am . . .	**Ben . . .**
	behn
from London	**Londra'dan**
	l*o*hn-drah-dahn

from England	**İngiltere'den** een-gheel-teh-reh-dehn
from New York	**New York'tan** New York-tahn
from America	**Amerika'dan** ah-mehr-ree-kah-dahn
from the north	**kuzeyden** koo-zehy-dehn
from the south	**güneyden** gooh-nehy-dehn
from the east	**doğudan** doh-oo-dahn
from the west	**batıdan** bah-tuh-dahn
from the centre	**ortadan** ohr-tah-dahn

[*For other countries, see p. 127*]

For the businessman and woman

I'm from . . . (firm's name)	**Ben . . .** (firm's name) **'denim** ben (. . .)-deh-neem
I have an appointment with . . .	(person's name) **. . . ile randevum var** (. . .) ee-leh rahn-deh-voom vahr
May I speak to . . .?	(person's name) **. . . ile görüşebilir miyim?** (. . .) ee-leh ger-oohsh-eh-bee-leer mee-yeem
This is my card	**İşte kartım** eesh-teh kahr-tuhm
I'm sorry I'm late	**Geç kaldığım için özür dilerim** ghech kahl-duh-uhm ee-cheen er-zoohr dee-leh-reem
Can I fix another appointment?	**Başka bir randevu alabilir miyim?** bahsh-kah beer rahn-deh-voo ah-lah-bee-leer mee-yeem
I'm staying at the (Hilton) hotel	**(Hilton) otelinde kalıyorum** (heel-tohn) oh-teh-leen-deh kah-luh-yoh-room
I'm staying in (Meşrutiyet) Avenue	**(Meşrutiyet) Caddesinde kalıyorum** (mehsh-roo-tee-yeht) jahd-deh-seen-deh kah-luh-yoh-room

Asking directions

ESSENTIAL INFORMATION

- Keep a look-out for all these place names as you will find them on shops, maps and notices.

WHAT TO SAY

Excuse me, please	**Affedersiniz, efendim** ahf-feh-dehr-see-neez eh-fehn-deem
How do I get . . .	**. . . nasıl gidebilirim?** nah-suhl ghee-deh-bee-lee-reem
to Ankara?	**Ankara'ya** ahn-kah-rah-yah
to Istanbul?	**İstanbul'a** ee-stahn-boo-lah
to (Cumhuriyet) Avenue?	**(Cumhuriyet) Caddesine** (juhm-hoo-ree-yeht) jahd-deh-see-neh
to the (Pera Palas) hotel?	**(Pera Palas) oteline** (peh-rah pah-lahs) oh-teh-lee-neh
to the airport?	**Hava meydanına** hah-vah mey-dah-nuh-nah
to the beach?	**Plaja** plah-zhah
to the bus station?	**Otobüs durağına** oh-toh-boohs doo-rah-uh-nah
to the historic site?	**Tarihi yere** tah-ree-hee yeh-reh
to the police station?	**Karakola** kah-rah-koh-lah
to the port?	**Limana** lee-mah-nah
to the (ferry) landing?	**İskeleye** ees-keh-leh-yeh
to the post office?	**Postaneye** poh-stah-neh-yeh
to the railway station?	**İstasyona** ee-stahs-yoh-nah

to the sports stadium?	**Stadyuma** stahd-yoo-mah
to the tourist information office?	**Danışma bürosuna** dah-nuhsh-mah booh-roh-soo-nah
to the town centre?	**Şehir merkezine** sheh-heer mehr-keh-zee-neh
to the town hall?	**Belediye dairesine** beh-leh-dee-yeh dy-reh-see-neh
Excuse me	**Affedersiniz** ahf-feh-dehr-see-neez
Is there . . . nearby?	**Civarda . . . var mı?** jee-vahr-dah . . . vahr muh
an art gallery	**bir sanat galerisi** beer sah-naht gah-leh-ree-see
a baker's	**bir fırıncı** beer fuh-ruhn-juh
a bank	**bir banka** beer bahn-kah
a bar	**bir bar** beer bahr
a bus stop	**bir otobüs durağı** beer oh-toh-boohs doo-rah-uh
a butcher's	**bir kasap** beer kah-sahp
a café	**bir kafe** beer kah-feh
a cake shop	**bir pastane** beer pah-stah-neh
a campsite	**bir kamp yeri** beer kahmp yeh-ree
a car park	**bir park** beer pahrk
a change bureau	**bir kambiyo** beer kahm-bee-yoh
a chemist's	**bir eczane** beer ehj-zah-neh
a church	**bir kilise** beer kee-lee-seh
a cinema	**bir sinema** beer see-neh-mah
a concert hall	**bir konser salonu** beer kohn-sehr sah-loh-noo

a delicatessen	**bir şarküteri**
	beer shah-kooh-teh-r*ee*
a dentist	**bir dişçi**
	beer deesh-ch*ee*
a department store	**bir büyuk mağaza**
	bir booh-y*oo*hk mah-ah-z*a*h
a disco	**bir diskotek**
	beer dees-koh-t*e*hk
a doctor	**bir doktor**
	beer dohk-t*o*hr
a dry cleaner's	**bir kuru temizleyici**
	beer koo-roo teh-meez-leh-yee-j*ee*
a fishmonger's	**bir balıkçı**
	beer bah-luhk-ch*uh*
a garage (for repairs)	**bir tamirhane**
	beer tah-meer-hah-n*eh*
a hairdresser's	**bir kuaför**
	beer kwah-f*e*r
a greengrocer's	**bir manav**
	beer mah-n*a*hv
a grocer's	**bir bakkal**
	beer bahk-k*a*hl
a hardware shop	**bir hırdavatçı**
	beer huhr-dah-vaht-ch*u*h
a hospital	**bir hastane**
	beer hah-st*a*h-neh
a hotel	**bir otel**
	beer *o*h-tehl
a laundry	**bir çamaşırhane**
	beer chah-mah-sh*u*hr-hah-neh
a mosque	**bir cami**
	beer jah-m*ee*
a museum	**bir müze**
	beer mooh-z*e*h
a newsagent's	**bir gazeteci**
	beer gah-zeh-teh-j*ee*
a nightclub	**bir gece kulübü**
	beer gheh-jeh koo-looh-b*oo*h
a park	**bir park**
	beer pahrk
a petrol station	**bir benzin deposu**
	beer behn-z*ee*n deh-poh-s*oo*

Is there . . . nearby?	**Civarda . . . var mi?**
	jee-vahr-d*ah* . . . vahr muh
a postbox	**bir posta kutusu**
	beer poh-stah koo-too-s*oo*
a restaurant	**bir lokanta**
	beer loh-k*ah*n-tah
a sports ground	**bir spor alanı**
	beer spohr ah-lah-n*uh*
a supermarket	**bir süpermarket**
	beer sooh-pehr-mahr-k*e*ht
a sweet shop	**bir şekerci**
	beer sheh-kehr-j*ee*
a swimming pool	**bir yüzme havuzu**
	beer yoohz-m*e*h hah-voo-z*oo*
a synagogue	**bir sinagog**
	beer see-nah-g*oh*g
a taxi stand	**bir taksi durağı**
	beer tahk-s*ee* doo-rah-*uh*
a telephone	**bir telefon**
	beer teh-leh-f*oh*n
a theatre	**bir tiyatro**
	beer tee-y*ah*-troh
a tobacconist's	**bir tütüncü**
	beer tooh-toohn-j*oo*
a toilet	**bir tuvalet**
	beer too-wah-l*e*t
a travel agent	**bir turizm acentası**
	beer too-r*ee*zm ah-jehn-tah-s*uh*
a zoo	**bir hayvanat bahçesi**
	beer hy-vah-n*ah*t bah-cheh-s*ee*

DIRECTIONS

- Asking where a place is, or if a place is nearby, is one thing; making sense of the answer is another.
- Here are some of the most important key directions and replies.

Left	**Sol**
	sohl
Right	**Sağ**
	sah

Straight on	**Düz**
	doohz
There	**Oraya/Orada**
	oh-rah-yah/oh-rah-dah
First (left/right)	**(Soldan/Sağdan) birinci**
	(sohl-dahn/sah-dahn) bee-reen-jee
Second (left/right)	**(Soldan/Sağdan) ikinci**
	(sohl-dahn/sah-dahn) ee-keen-jee
At the crossroads	**Kavşakta**
	kahv-shahk-tah
At the roundabout	**Dönel kavşakta**
	der-nehl kahv-shahk-tah
At the traffic lights	**Trafik lambasında**
	trah-feek lahm-bah-suhn-dah
It's near/far	**Yakın/uzak**
	yah-kuhn/oo-zahk
One kilometre	**Bir kilometre**
	beer kee-loh-meh-treh
Two kilometres	**İki kilometre**
	ee-kee kee-loh-meh-treh
Five minutes . . .	**Beş dakika**
	behsh dah-kee-kah
on foot	**yaya**
	yah-yah
by car	**araba ile**
	ah-rah-bah ee-leh
Take . . .	**. . . bininiz**
	bee-nee-neez
the bus	**Otobüse**
	oh-toh-booh-seh
the ferryboat	**Vapura**
	vah-poo-rah
the train	**Trene**
	treh-neh
the **dolmuş**	**Dolmuşa**
	dohl-moo-shah

[*For public transport, see p. 105*]

The tourist information office

ESSENTIAL INFORMATION

- All the main towns in Turkey, and many of the smaller ones, have tourist information offices. There are also information desks at airports and border crossings. There will usually be someone there who speaks English.
- Look out for this symbol:

and the following sign:

İ

DANIŞMA BÜROSU (information office)
- These offices can give you free information in the form of printed leaflets, fold-outs, brochures, maps, lists and plans.
- For finding a tourist office, see p. 17.

WHAT TO SAY

Please, have you got . . .	**Lütfen, . . . var mı?**
	looht-fehn . . . vahr muh
a plan of the town?	**bir şehir planı**
	beer sheh-heer plah-nuh
a list of hotels?	**bir otel listesi**
	beer oh-tehl lees-teh-see
a list of campsites?	**bir kamp listesi**
	beer kahmp lees-teh-see
a list of restaurants?	**bir lokanta listesi**
	beer loh-kahn-tah lees-teh-see
a list of events?	**bir önemli olaylar listesi**
	beer er-nehm-lee oh-ly-lahr lees-teh-see
a leaflet on the town?	**şehir hakkında bir broşür**
	sheh-heer hahk-kuhn-dah beer broh-shoohr
a leaflet on the region?	**bölge hakkında bir broşür**
	berl-gheh hahk-kuhn-dah beer broh-shoohr
a railway timetable?	**bir tren tarifesi**
	beer trehn tah-ree-feh-see

a bus timetable?	**bir otobüs tarifesi** beer oh-toh-boohs tah-ree-feh-see
In English, please	**İngilizçe, lütfen** een-ghee-leez-cheh loot-fehn
Can you recommend . . .	**. . . tavsiye edebilir misiniz?** tahv-see-yeh eh-deh-bee-leer mee-see-neez
a (cheap) hotel?	**(Ucuz) Bir otel** (oo-jooz) beer oh-tehl
a (cheap) restaurant?	**(Ucuz) Bir lokanta** (oo-jooz) beer loh-kahn-tah
Can you book a (room/table) for me?	**Bir (oda/masa) rezervasyonu yapabilir misiniz?** beer (oh-dah/mah-sah) reh-zehr-vahs-yoh-nooh yah-pah-bee-leer mee-see-neez

LIKELY ANSWERS

You need to understand when the answer is 'No'. You should be able to tell by the assistant's facial expression, tone of voice and gesture; but there are some language clues, such as:

No	**Hayır** hah-yuhr
There isn't/aren't any . . .	**. . . yok** yohk
I'm sorry	**Özür dilerim** er-zoohr dee-leh-reem
I don't have a list of campsites	**Kamp listesi yok** kahmp lees-teh-see yohk
I haven't got any left	**Kalmamış** kahl-mah-muhsh
It's free	**Bedava** beh-dah-vah

Accommodations

Hotel

ESSENTIAL INFORMATION

- If you want hotel-type accommodation, all the following words in capital letters are worth looking for on name boards:
  OTEL
  MOTEL
  PANSİYON (a small family hotel)
- A list of hotels in the town can usually be obtained at the local tourist office [see p. 22].
- Hotels are officially classified into five categories: luxury, then classes 1 to 4. Some medium-class hotels can be as good as, or even better than, those in higher categories.
- The cost is displayed in the room itself so you can check it when having a look around before agreeing to stay.
- The displayed cost is for the room itself, per night, and not per person. Breakfast is sometimes included. A Turkish breakfast consists of eggs, white cheese, olives, bread and jam or honey, with tea, coffee or milk.
- Service is included in the bill but tipping of the staff, especially after a long stay, is usual.
- Your passport is requested when registering.
- For finding a hotel, see p. 17.

WHAT TO SAY

I have a booking	**Rezervasyonum var**
	reh-zehr-vahs-yoh-noom vahr
Have you any rooms, please?	**Odanız var mı?**
	oh-dah-nuhz vahr muh
Can I book a room?	**Rezervasyon yapabiliyor muyum?**
	reh-zehr-vahs-yohn yah-pah-bee-lee-yohr muh-yuhm

For one person	**Tek kişilik** tehk kee-shee-l*ee*k
For two people	**İki kişilik** ee-k*ee* kee-shee-l*ee*k
[*For numbers, see p. 118*] For . . .	**. . . için** ee-ch*ee*n
one night	**Bir gece** beer gheh-j*e*h
two nights	**İki gece** ee-k*ee* gheh-jeh
one week	**Bir hafta** beer hahf-t*a*h
two weeks	**İki hafta** ee-k*ee* hahf-t*a*h
I would like . . .	**. . . istiyorum** ees-t*ee*-yoh-room
a room	**Bir oda** beer oh-d*a*h
two rooms	**İki oda** ee-k*ee* oh-d*a*h
with a single bed	**tek yataklı** tehk yah-tahk-l*u*h
with two single beds	**çift yataklı** cheeft yah-tahk-l*u*h
with a double bed	**iki kişilik yataklı** ee-k*ee* kee-shee-l*ee*k yah-tahk-l*u*h
with a toilet	**tuvaletli** too-wah-leht-l*ee*
with a bathroom	**banyolu** bahn-yoh-l*oo*
with a shower	**duşlu** doosh-l*oo*
with a cot	**çocuk yatağı ile** choh-j*oo*k yah-tah-*u*h ee-leh
with a balcony	**balkonlu** bahl-kohn-l*oo*
Do you serve meals?	**Yemek servisi yapıyor musunuz?** yeh-m*e*hk sehr-vee-s*ee* yah-p*u*h-yohr moo-soo-n*oo*z
At what time is . . .	**Saat kaçta . . .** sah-*a*ht kahch-t*a*h

breakfast?

kahvaltı?
kah-vahl-t*u*h

lunch?

öğle yemeği?
er-leh yeh-meh-*ee*

dinner?

akşam yemeği?
ahk-shahm yeh-meh-*ee*

How much is it?

Ne kadar?
neh kah-d*a*hr

Can I look at the room?

Odaya bakabilir miyim?
oh-dah-y*a*h bah-kah-bee-l*ee*r mee-yeem

I'd prefer a room . . .

. . . bir oda tercih ederim
beer oh-d*a*h tehr-j*ee* eh-deh-r*ee*m

at the front/at the back

Ön tarafta/Arka tarafta
ern tah-rahf-t*a*h/ahr-k*a*h tah-rahf-tah

OK, I'll take it

Tamam, bunu tutarım
tah-m*a*hm boo-n*oo* too-tah-r*u*hm

No thanks, I won't take it

Teşekkürler, bunu istemiyorum
teh-shehk-koohr-l*e*hr boo-n*oo* ees-teh-mee-yoh-room

The key to number (10), please

Oda anahtarı, numara (on), lütfen
oh-d*a*h ah-nah-tah-r*u*h noo-mah-rah (ohn) l*oo*ht-fehn

Please may I have . . .

Lütfen, . . . veriniz
l*oo*ht-fehn . . . veh-ree-n*ee*z

a coat hanger

bir askı
beer ahs-k*u*h

a towel

bir havlu
bee hahv-l*oo*

a glass

bir bardak
beer bahr-d*a*hk

some soap

sabun
sah-b*oo*n

an ashtray

bir küllük
beer koohl-l*oo*hk

another pillow

bir yastık daha
beer yahs-t*u*hk dah-h*a*h

another blanket

bir battaniye daha
beer baht-t*a*h-nee-yeh dah-h*a*h

Come in!

Buyurun!
boo-yoo-r*oo*n

One moment, please	**Bir dakika, lütfen**
	beer dah-*kee*-kah *loo*ht-fehn
Please (would you) . . .	**Lütfen** . . .
	*loo*ht-fehn
do this laundry	**bu çamaşırı yıkayınız**
	boo chah-mah-sh*uh*-ruh yah-kah-yuh-n*uh*z
do this dry cleaning	**bunu kuru temizlemeye veriniz**
	boo-n*oo* koo-r*oo* teh-meez-leh-meh-yeh veh-ree-n*ee*z
call me at (6) o'clock	**saat (altı) da bana haber veriniz**
	sah-*a*ht (ahl-t*uh*) d*a*h bah-n*a*h hah-b*e*hr veh-ree-n*ee*z
help me with my luggage	**bagajıma yardım ediniz**
	bah-gah-zhuh-m*a*h yahr-d*u*hm eh-dee-n*ee*z
call me a taxi for (7) o'clock	**saat (yedi) için bir taksi çağırınız**
	sah-*a*ht (yeh-d*ee*) ee-ch*ee*n beer tahk-s*ee* chah-uh-ruh-n*uh*z
[*For times, see p. 120*]	
The bill, please	**Hesabı, lütfen**
	heh-sah-b*uh loo*ht-fehn
Is service included?	**Servis dahil mi?**
	sehr-v*ee*s dah-h*ee*l mee
I think this is wrong	**Bir yanlışlık var galiba**
	beer yahn-luhsh-l*u*hk vahr g*a*h-lee-bah
May I have a receipt	**Bir makbuz veriniz**
	beer mahk-b*oo*z veh-ree-n*ee*z

At breakfast

Some more . . . please	**Biraz daha . . . lütfen**
	bee-r*a*hz dah-h*a*h . . . *loo*ht-fehn
coffee	**kahve**
	kah-v*e*h
tea	**çay**
	chay
bread	**ekmek**
	ehk-m*e*hk
butter	**tereyağ**
	teh-reh-y*a*h

jam/honey	**reçel/bal** reh-ch*eh*l/bahl
A boiled egg, please	**Bir kaynamış yumurta, lütfen** beer kay-nah-m*uh*sh yoo-moor-t*ah* l*oo*ht-fehn

LIKELY REACTIONS

Have you an identity document, please?	**Hüviyetiniz var mı, lütfen?** hooh-vee-yeh-tee-n*eez* vahr muh l*oo*ht-fehn
What's your name?	**Adınız ne?** ah-duh-n*uh*z neh
Sorry, we're full	**Özür dilerim, doluyuz** er-z*oo*hr dee-leh-r*ee*m doh-loo-yooz
We have no rooms	**Odamız yok** oh-dah-m*uh*z yohk
Do you want to have a look?	**Bakmak ister misiniz?** Bahk-m*ah*k ees-t*eh*r mee-see-n*eez*
How many people is it for?	**Kaç kişi için** kahch kee-sh*ee* ee-ch*ee*n
From (7) o'clock onwards	**Saat (yedi)den sonra** sah-*ah*t (yeh-dee)dehn s*oh*n-rah
From (midday) onwards	**(Öğleden) sonra** (er-leh-dehn) s*oh*n-rah
[For times, see p. 120] It's (10,000) lira	**(On bin) lira** (ohn been) l*ee*-rah

[For numbers, see p. 118]

Camping and youth hosteling

ESSENTIAL INFORMATION

Camping

● Look for the words **KAMP** or **CAMPING** and signs like these:

- Be prepared to have to pay
  per person
  for the car (if applicable)
  for the tent or caravan plot
  for electricity
  for hot showers
- You must provide proof of identity, such as your passport.
- You can obtain information on campsites from local tourist offices.
- There are camping sites throughout Turkey, including some good ones in or near the main cities and tourist attractions. Camping off site is also possible, though one should try to ask permission of the landowner. Camping in very remote places is not advisable.

Youth hostels

- Because of the general availability of low-cost accommodation there are few hostels in Turkey. Those that do exist are essentially student hostels with shared facilities. None of them requires an IYHF (International Youth Hostel Federation) card, though some offer cardholders 10–20% discounts.

WHAT TO SAY

I have a booking	**Rezervasyonum var** reh-zehr-vahs-yoh-n*oo*m vahr
Have you any space?	**Boş yeriniz var mı?** bohsh yeh-ree-n*ee*z vahr muh
It's for . . .	**. . . için** ee-ch*ee*n
one person	**Bir tek kişi** beer tehk kee-sh*ee*
two people	**İki kişi** ee-k*ee* kee-sh*ee*
and one child	**ve bir çocuk** veh beer choh-j*oo*k
and two children	**ve iki çocuk** veh ee-k*ee* choh-jook
It's for . . .	**. . . için** ee-ch*ee*n
one night	**Bir tek gece** beer tehk gheh-j*eh*
two nights	**İki gece** ee-k*ee* gheh-j*eh*

one week
Bir hafta
beer hahf-t*ah*

two weeks
İki hafta
ee-k*ee* hahf-t*ah*

How much is it . . .
. . . ne kadar?
neh kah-d*ah*r

for the tent?
Çadır
chah-d*uh*r

for the caravan?
Karavan
kah-rah-v*ah*n

for the car?
Araba
ah-rah-b*ah*

for the electricity?
Elektrik
eh-lehk-tr*ee*k

per person?
Kişi için
kee-sh*ee* ee-ch*ee*n

per night?
Gece için
gheh-ch*eh* ee-ch*ee*n

May I look round?
Bakabilir miyim?
bah-kah-bee-l*ee*r mee-y*ee*m

At what time do you lock up at night?
Saat kaçta kapayı kilitliyorsunuz?
sah-*ah*ht kahch-t*ah* kah-pah-y*uh* kee-leet-lee-yohr-soo-n*ooz*

Is there anything . . .
. . . var mı?
vahr muh

to eat?
Yemek
yeh-m*eh*k

to drink?
İçecek
ee-cheh-j*eh*k

Is/are there . . .
. . . var mı?
vahr muh

a bar?
Bar
bahr

hot showers?
Sıcak duşlar
suh-j*ah*k doosh-l*ah*r

a kitchen?
Mutfak
moot-f*ah*k

a laundry?
Çamaşırhane
chah-mah-sh*uh*r-hah-neh

a restaurant?
Lokanta
loh-k*ah*n-tah

a shop?	**Dükkân** doohk-k*a*hn
a swimming pool?	**Yüzme havuzu** yoohz-m*e*h h*a*h-voo-z*oo*

[*For food shopping, see p. 53, and for eating and drinking out, see p. 72*]

Where are . . .	**. . . nerede?** n*e*h-reh-d*e*h
the dustbins?	**Çöp kutuları** cherp koo-too-lah-r*u*h
the showers?	**Duşlar** doosh-l*a*hr
the toilets?	**Tuvaletler** too-wah-leht-l*e*hr
Please have you got . . .	**Lütfen . . . var mı?** l*oo*ht-fehn . . . vahr muh
a broom?	**süpürge** sooh-poohr-gh*e*h
a corkscrew?	**tirbuşon** teer-boo-sh*o*hn
a drying-up cloth?	**kurulama bezi** koo-roo-lah-m*a*h beh-z*ee*
a fork?	**çatal** chah-t*a*hl
a fridge?	**buzdolabı** booz-doh-lah-b*u*h
a frying pan?	**tava** tah-v*a*h
an iron?	**ütü** ooh-t*oo*h
a knife?	**bıçak** buh-ch*a*hk
a plate?	**tabak** tah-b*a*hk
a saucepan?	**tencere** t*e*hn-jeh-reh
a teaspoon?	**çay kaşığı** chay kah-shuh-*u*h
a tin-opener?	**konserve açacağı** kohn-s*e*hr-veh ah-chah-jah-*u*h
washing powder?	**çamaşır tozu** chah-mah-sh*u*hr toh-z*oo*

washing-up liquid?

bulaşık deterjanı
boo-lah-shuhk deh-tehr-jah-nuh

The bill, please

Hesabı, lütfen
heh-sah-buh looht-fehn

Problems

The toilet

Tuvalet
too-wah-leht

The shower

Duş
doosh

The tap

Musluk
moos-look

The razor point

Traş makinası için priz
trahsh mah-kee-nah-suh ee-cheen preez

The light

Işık
uh-shuhk

. . . is not working

. . . yanmıyor
yahn-muh-yohr

My camping gas has run out

Bütan gazım bitmiş
booh-tahn gah-zuhm beet-meesh

LIKELY REACTIONS

Have you an identity document, please?

Hüviyetiniz var mı, lütfen?
hooh-vee-yeh-tee-neez vahr muh looht-fehn

What's your name?

Adınız ne?
ah-duh-nuhz neh

Sorry, we're full

Özür dilerim, doluyuz
er-zoohr dee-leh-reem doh-loo-yooz

How many people is it for?

Kaç kişi için
kahch kee-shee ee-cheen

How many nights is it for?

Kaç gece için
kahch gheh-jeh ee-cheen

It's (8,000) lira

(Sekiz bin) lira
(seh-keez been) lee-rah

[For numbers, see p. 118]

Rented accommodations: problem solving

ESSENTIAL INFORMATION

- If you are looking for accommodation to rent, look out for these words:
  KİRALIK (for rent)
  APARTMAN DAİRESİ (apartment, flat)
- For arranging your let, see 'Hotel', p. 24.
- Key words you will meet if renting on the spot:
  Depozito (deposit)
  deh-poh-*zee*-toh
  Anahtar (key)
  ah-nah-t*a*hr
- Having arranged your own accommodation and arrived with the key, check the obvious basics that you take for granted at home.
  Electricity: voltage? Usually the supply is 240v, but there are some districts where it is 110v, so razors and small appliances brought from home may need adjusting. For razors and appliances with three-point plugs it is well worth bringing adaptors from home to fit the two-point continental sockets that are universal.
  Cooker: there may not be an oven, and don't be surprised to find:
  – a lid covering the rings which lifts up to form a splashback
  – a mixture of gas and electric rings.
  Toilet: Turkish plumbing blocks easily, so do not throw things in the toilet. Some toilets cannot take toilet paper – if so a bin is provided beside the lavatory to dispose of it.
  Water: find the stopcock. Check taps and plugs – they may not operate in the way you are used to. Check how to turn on (or light) the hot water.
  Windows: check the method of opening and closing the windows and shutters.
  Insects: is an insecticide spray provided? If not, get one locally.
  Equipment: for buying or replacing equipment, see p. 48.
- You will probably have an official agent, but be clear in your own mind whom to contact in an emergency, even if it is only a neighbour in the first place.

WHAT TO SAY

My name is . . .	**Adım . . .**
	ah-du*hm*
I'm staying at . . .	**. . . 'da kalıyorum**
	. . . dah kah-lu*h*-yoh-room
The . . . has been cut off	**. . . kesilmiş**
	keh-seel-m*ee*sh
electricity	**Elektrik**
	eh-lehk-tr*ee*k
gas	**Havagazı**
	hah-v*a*h-gah-zuh
water	**Su**
	soo
Is there . . . in the area?	**Civarda . . . var mı?**
	jee-vahr-d*a*h . . . vahr muh
an electrician	**elektrikçi**
	eh-lehk-tr*ee*k-ch*ee*
a plumber	**borucu**
	boh-roo-j*oo*
a gas fitter	**havagazı ustası**
	hah-v*a*h-gah-zuh oos-tah-s*u*h
Where is . . .	**. . . nerede?**
	neh-reh-d*e*h
the fusebox?	**Sigorta**
	see-g*o*hr-tah
the stopcock? (water main)	**Su vanası**
	soo vah-nah-s*u*h
the boiler?	**Kazan**
	kah-z*a*hn
the (electric) water heater?	**Termosifon**
	tehr-moh-see-f*o*hn
Is there . . .	**. . . var mı?**
	vahr muh
town gas?	**Havagazı**
	hah-v*a*h-gah-zuh
bottled gas?	**Bütan gazı**
	boo-t*a*hn gah-z*u*h
central heating?	**Kalorifer**
	kah-loh-ree-f*e*hr
The cooker	**Ocak**
	oh-j*a*hk

The hair dryer	**Saç kurutuma makinası** sahch koo-roo-too-mah mah-kee-nah-suh
The heating	**Kalorifer** kah-loh-ree-fehr
The immersion heater	**Termosifon** tehr-moh-see-fohn
The iron	**Ütü** ooh-tooh
The pilot light	**Pilot** pee-loht
The refrigerator	**Buzdolabı** booz-doh-lah-buh
The telephone	**Telefon** teh-leh-fohn
The washing machine	**Çamaşır makinası** chah-mah-shuhr mah-kee-nah-suh
The (electric) water heater	**Termosifon** tehr-moh-see-fohn
. . . is not working	**. . . işlemiyor** ish-leh-mee-yohr
Where can I get . . .	**. . . nerede bulabilirim?** neh-reh-deh boo-lah-bee-lee-reem
an adaptor for this?	**Bunun için bir adaptör** boo-noon ee-cheen beer ah-dahp-ter
a bottle of butane gas?	**Bir tüp bütan gazı** beer toohp booh-tahn gah-zuh
a fuse?	**Bir sigorta** beer see-gohr-tah
an insecticide spray?	**Böcek öldürücüsü** ber-jehk erl-dooh-rooh-jooh-sooh
a light bulb?	**Bir ampul** beer ahm-pool
The drain	**Pis su borusu** pees soo boh-ruh-soo
The sink	**Eviye** eh-vee-yeh
The toilet	**Tuvalet** too-wah-leht
. . . is blocked	**. . . tıkalı** tuh-kah-luh

The gas is leaking	**Gazı kaçak yapıyor**
	gah-zuh kah-chahk yah-puh-yohr
Can you mend it straightaway?	**Hemen tamir edebilir misiniz?**
	heh-mehn tah-meer eh-deh-bee-leer
	mee-see-neez
When can you mend it?	**Ne zaman tamir edebilir siniz?**
	neh zah-mahn tah-meer eh-deh-
	bee-leer see-neez
How much do I owe you?	**Borcum ne kadar?**
	bohr-joom neh kah-dahr
When is the rubbish collected?	**Çöp ne zaman toplanıyor?**
	cherp neh zah-mahn toh-plah-nuh-
	yohr

LIKELY REACTIONS

What's your name?	**Adınız ne?**
	ah-duh-nuhz neh
What's your address?	**Adresiniz ne?**
	ah-dreh-see-neez neh
There's a shop . . .	**. . . dükkân var**
	doohk-kahn vahr
in town	**Şehirde**
	sheh-heer-deh
in the village	**Köyde**
	ker-yee-deh
I can't come . . .	**. . . gelemiyorum**
	gheh-leh-mee-yoh-room
today	**Bugün**
	boo-goohn
this week	**Bu hafta**
	boo hahf-tah
until Monday	**Pazartesinden önce**
	pah-zahr-teh-seen-dehn ern-jeh
I can come . . .	**. . . gelebiliyorum**
	gheh-leh-bee-lee-yoh-room
on Tuesday	**Salı günü**
	sah-luh gooh-nooh
when you want	**Her ne zaman isterseniz**
	hehr neh zah-mahn ees-tehr-seh-
	neez

Every day	**Her gün**
	hehr goohn
Every other day	**İki günde bir**
	ee-*kee* goohn-deh beer
On Wednesdays	**Çarşamba günleri**
	chahr-shahm-b*ah* goohn-leh-r*ee*

[*For days of the week, see p. 122*]

General shopping

The pharmacy/The chemist's

ESSENTIAL INFORMATION

- Look out for this word:
  ECZANE (chemist)
  NÖBETÇİ ECZANE (duty chemist)
- Chemists are easy to find, open until about 8.00 p.m., and in each district take it in turns to stay open throughout the night and during holidays. The name and address of the nearest duty chemist is displayed in the window of every chemist shop.
- Many drugs available only on prescription in the UK can be bought over the counter in Turkey.
- For finding a chemist, see p. 17.

WHAT TO SAY

I'd like . . .	**. . . istiyorum**
	ees-*tee*-yoh-room
some aspirin	**Aspirin**
	ahs-pee-r*ee*n

some antiseptic	**Antiseptik**
	ahn-tee-sehp-*tee*k
some bandage	**Sargı**
	sahr-g*uh*
some cotton wool	**Pamuk**
	pah-m*oo*k
some eye drops	**Göz damlası**
	gherz dahm-lah-s*uh*
some foot powder	**Ayak pudrası**
	ah-yahk poo-drah-s*uh*
some gauze dressing	**Gazlı bez**
	gahz-l*uh* behz
some inhalant	**İnhalatör**
	een-hah-lah-t*er*
some insect repellent	**Böcek kremi**
	ber-jehk kreh-m*ee*
some lip salve	**Dudak kremi**
	doo-d*a*hk kreh-m*ee*
some nose drops	**Burun damlası**
	boo-r*oo*n dahm-lah-s*uh*
some sticking plaster	**Plaster**
	plah-st*e*hr
some throat pastilles	**Boğaz pastili**
	boh-*a*hz pahs-tee-l*ee*
some Vaseline	**Vazelin**
	vah-zeh-l*ee*n
I'd like something for . . .	**. . . için bir şey istiyorum**
	ee-ch*ee*n beer shehy ees-t*ee*-yoh-room
(insect) bites	**Böcek ısırığı**
	ber-j*e*hk uh-suh-ruh-*uh*
burns	**Yanık**
	yah-n*uh*k
chilblains	**Mayasıl**
	mah-yah-s*uh*l
a cold	**Nezle**
	nehz-*le*h
constipation	**Kabızlık**
	kah-buhz-l*uh*k
a cough	**Öksürük**
	erk-sooh-r*oo*hk
diarrhoea	**İshal**
	ees-h*a*hl

earache	**Kulak ağrısı**
	koo-lahk ah-ruh-suh
flu	**Grip**
	greep
scalds	**Yanık**
	yah-nuhk
sore gums	**Dişeti ağrısı**
	deesh-eh-tee ah-ruh-suh
sprains	**Burkulma**
	boor-kool-mah
stings	**Sokma**
	sohk-mah
sunburn	**Güneş yanığı**
	gooh-nehsh yah-nuh-uh
car/sea/air/travel sickness	**Araba/Deniz/Hava/Yol tutması**
	ah-rah-bah/deh-neez/hah-vah/yohl
	toot-mah-suh
I need . . .	**. . . istiyorum**
	ees-tee-yoh-room
some baby food	**Mama**
	mah-mah
some contraceptives	**Preservatif**
	preh-sehr-vah-teef
some deodorant	**Deodoran**
	deh-oh-doh-rahn
some (disposable) nappies	**Çocuk bezi**
	choh-jook beh-zee
some hand cream	**El kremi**
	ehl kreh-mee
some lipstick	**Ruj**
	roozh
some make-up remover	**Makyaj silme**
	mahk-yahzh seel-meh
some paper tissues	**Kağıt mendil**
	kah-uht mehn-deel
some razor blades	**Tıraş bıçağı**
	tuh-rahsh buh-chah-uh
some safety pins	**Çengelli iğne**
	chehn-ghehl-lee ee-neh
some sanitary towels	**Hijenik bez**
	hee-zheh-neek behz
some shaving cream	**Tıraş kremi**
	tuh-rahsh kreh-mee

some soap	**Sabun**
	sah-b*oo*n
some suntan lotion/oil	**Güneş kremi/yağı**
	gooh-n*e*hsh kreh-m*ee*/yah-*u*h
some talcum powder	**Talk pudrası**
	tahlk poo-drah-s*u*h
some Tampax	**Tampaks**
	tahm-p*a*hks
some toilet paper	**Tuvalet kağıdı**
	too-wah-l*e*ht kah-uh-d*u*h
some toothpaste	**Diş macunu**
	deesh mah-joo-n*oo*

[*For other essential expressions, see 'Shop talk', p. 50*]

Vacation items

ESSENTIAL INFORMATION

- Places to shop at and signs to look for:
  FOTOĞRAFÇI (photographer)
  KIRTASİYECİ (stationer)
  KİTABEVİ (bookshop)
  TÜTÜNCÜ (tobacconist)

WHAT TO SAY

Where can I buy . . .	**. . . nerede alabiliyorum?**
	neh-reh-d*e*h ah-lah-bee-l*ee*-yoh-room
a bag?	**Bir çanta**
	beer ch*a*hn-tah
a beach ball?	**Plaj için bir top**
	plahzh ee-ch*ee*n beer tohp
a bucket?	**Bir kova**
	beer koh-v*ah*

an English newspaper?	**İngilizce gazete** een-ghee-leez-jeh gah-zeh-teh
some envelopes?	**Zarf** zahrf
a guide book?	**Bir rehber** beer reh-behr
a map?	**Bir harita** beer hah-ree-tah
some postcards?	**Kartpostal** kahrt-pohs-tahl
a spade?	**Bir bel** beer behl
a straw hat?	**Bir hasır şapka** beer hah-suhr shahp-kah
a suitcase?	**Bir valiz** beer vah-leez
some sunglasses?	**Güneş gözlüğü** gooh-nehsh gerz-looh-ooh
a sunshade?	**Bir şemsiye** beer shehm-see-yeh
some writing paper?	**Yazı kâğıdı** yah-zuh kah-uh-duh
I'd like . . . [*show the camera*]	**. . . istiyorum** ees-tee-yoh-room
a colour film	**Renkli filim** rehn-klee fee-leem
a black and white film	**Siyah-beyaz filim** see-yah-beh-yahz fee-leem
for prints	**baskı için** bahs-kuh ee-cheen
for slides	**slayt için** slahyt ee-cheen
12(24/36) exposures	**on iki (yirmi dört/otuz altı) pozluk** ohn ee-kee (yeer-mee derrt/oh-tooz ahl-tuh) pohz-look
a standard 8mm film	**Standart sekiz milimetrelik filim** stahn-dahrt seh-keez mee-lee-meh-treh-leek fee-leem
a super 8 film	**Süper sekizlik filim** sooh-pehr seh-keez-leek fee-leem
some flash bulbs	**Flaş lambası** flahsh lahm-bah-suh

This camera is broken	**Bu fotoğraf makinası bozuk**
	boo foh-toh-r*a*hf mah-kee-nah-s*u*h
	boh-z*oo*k
The film is stuck	**Filim takıldı**
	fee-l*ee*m tah-kuhl-d*u*h
Please can you . . .	**Lütfen . . .**
	l*oo*ht-fehn
develop this?	**develop edebilir misiniz?**
	deh-veh-l*oh*p eh-deh-bee-l*ee*r mee-
	see-n*ee*z
print this	**basabilir misiniz?**
	bah-sah-bee-l*ee*r mee-see-n*ee*z
load the camera	**filim makinaya koyabilir misiniz?**
	fee-l*ee*m mah-kee-nah-y*a*h koh-
	yah-bee-l*ee*r mee-see-n*ee*z

[*For other essential expressions, see 'Shop talk', p. 50*]

The tobacco shop

ESSENTIAL INFORMATION

- The sign for tobacconists in Turkey is:
  TÜTÜNCÜ
- Tobacconists often sell newspapers, wine and spirits.
- Cigarettes can also be bought from street vendors.

WHAT TO SAY

A packet of cigarettes	**. . . bir paket sigara**
	beer pah-k*e*ht see-g*a*h-rah
with filters	**Filtreli**
	feel-treh-l*ee*
without filters	**Filtresiz**
	feel-treh-s*ee*z
menthol	**Mentollü**
	mehn-tohl-l*oo*h

A packet of kingsize cigarettes	**Bir paket uzun sigara**
	beer pah-keht oo-zoon see-gah-rah
Those up there . . .	**Şu üsttekileri . . .**
	shoo oohst-teh-kee-leh-ree
on the right	**sağda**
	sah-dah
on the left	**solda**
	sohl-dah
These [point]	**Şunlar**
	shoon-lahr
Cigarettes, please	**Sigara, lütfen**
	see-gah-rah looht-fehn
100/200/300	**Yüz/iki yüz/üç yüz**
	yoohz/ee-kee yoohz/oohch yoohz
Two packets	**İki paket**
	ee-kee pah-keht
Have you got . . .	**. . . var mı?**
	vahr muh
English cigarettes?	**İngiliz sigarası**
	een-ghee-leez see-gah-rah-suh
American cigarettes?	**Amerikan sigarası**
	ah-meh-ree-kahn see-gah-rah-suh
English pipe tobacco	**İngiliz pipo tütünü**
	een-ghee-leez pee-poh tooh-tooh-nooh
American pipe tobacco	**Amerikan pipo tütünü**
	ah-meh-ree-kahn pee-poh tooh-tooh-nooh
A packet of pipe tobacco	**Bir paket pipo tütünü**
	beer pah-keht pee-poh tooh-tooh-nooh
That one up there . . .	**Şu üsttekini . . .**
	shoo oohst-teh-kee-nee
on the right	**sağda**
	sah-dah
on the left	**solda**
	sohl-dah
That one [point]	**Şu**
	shoo
A cigar, please	**Bir puro**
	beer poo-roh
This one [point]	**Bu**
	booh

Some cigars, please	**Birkaç puro, lütfen**
	beer-kahch poo-roh looht-fehn
Those [point]	**Onlar**
	ohn-lahr
A box of matches	**Kibrit**
	kee-breet
A packet of pipe cleaners	**Bir paket pipo temizleyicisi**
	beer pah-keht pee-poh teh-meez-leh-yee-jee-see
A packet of flints [show lighter]	**Bir paket çakmak taşı**
	beer pah-keht chahk-mahk tah-shuh
Lighter fuel	**Çakmak benzini**
	chahk-mahk behn-zee-nee
Lighter gas, please	**Çakmak gazı, lütfen**
	chahk-mahk gah-zuh looht-fehn

[For other essential expressions, see 'Shop talk', p. 50]

Buying clothes

ESSENTIAL INFORMATION

- Look for:
  ELBİSE (clothing)
  GİYİM (clothing)
  GİYİMEVİ (clothing store)
- Don't buy without being measured first or without trying things on.
- Don't rely on conversion charts of clothing sizes [see p. 133].
- If you are buying for someone else, take their measurements with you.

WHAT TO SAY

I'd like . . .	. . . istiyorum
	ees-tee-yoh-room

an anorak	**Bir parka**
	beer pahr-kah
a belt	**Bir kemer**
	beer keh-mehr
a bikini	**Bir bikini**
	beer bee-kee-nee
a bra	**Bir sutyen**
	beer soot-yehn
a bathing cap	**Bir bone**
	beer boh-neh
a cardigan	**Bir hırka**
	beer huhr-kah
a coat	**Bir palto**
	beer pahl-toh
a dress	**Bir elbise**
	beer ehl-bee-seh
a hat	**Bir şapka**
	beer shahp-kah
a jacket	**Bir ceket**
	beer jeh-keht
a jumper	**Bir kazak**
	beer kah-zahk
a nightdress	**Bir gecelik**
	beer gheh-jeh-leek
a pullover	**Bir kazak**
	beer kah-zahk
some pyjamas	**Bir pijama**
	beer pee-jah-mah
a raincoat	**Bir yağmurluk**
	beer yah-moor-look
a shirt [for a woman]	**Bir bluz**
	beer blooz
a shirt [for a man]	**Bir gömlek**
	beer gherm-lehk
a skiing cap	**Bir ski şapkası**
	beer skee shahp-kah-suh
a skirt	**Bir etek**
	beer eh-tehk
a suit [for a woman]	**Bir tayör**
	beer tah-yer
a suit [for a man]	**Bir kostüm**
	beer kohs-toohm

a swimsuit	**Bir mayo**
	beer mah-yoh
some tights	**Bir külotlu çorap**
	beer kooh-loht-loo choh-rahp
some trousers	**Bir pantalon**
	beer pahn-tah-lohn
a T-shirt	**Bir tişort**
	beer tee-shohrt
I'd like . . .	**. . . istiyorum**
	ees-tee-yoh-room
a pair of briefs [for a woman]	**Bir külot**
	beer kooh-loht
a pair of gloves	**Eldivenler**
	ehl-dee-vehn-lehr
a pair of jeans	**Bir blucin**
	beer bloo-jeen
a pair of shorts	**Bir şort**
	beer shohrt
a pair of underpants [for a man]	**Bir külot**
	beer kooh-loht
I'd like a pair of . . .	**Bir çift . . . istiyorum**
	beer cheeft . . . ees-tee-yoh-room
(short/long) socks	**(kısa/uzun) çorap**
	(kuh-sah/oo-zoon) choh-rahp
stockings	**kadın çorabı**
	kah-duhn choh-rah-buh
shoes	**ayakkabı**
	ah-yahk-kah-buh
canvas shoes	**tenis ayakkabısı**
	teh-nees ah-yahk-kah-buh-suh
sandals	**sandal**
	sahn-dahl
boots	**çizme**
	cheez-meh
moccasins	**mokasen**
	moh-kah-sehn
slippers	**terlik**
	tehr-leek
I'd like a pair of beach shoes	**Plaj için bir çift ayakkabı istiyorum**
	plahzh ee-cheen beer cheeft ah-yahk-ah-buh ees-tee-yoh-room

The size is . . .	**. . . numarası** noo-mah-rah-s*uh*
[For numbers, see p. 118]	
Can you measure me, please?	**Ölçülerimi alır mısınız, lütfen?** erl-chooh-leh-ree-m*ee* ah-l*uh*r m*uh*-s*uh*-n*uh*z l*oo*ht-fehn
Can I try it on?	**Bunu deneyebilir miyim?** boo-n*oo* deh-neh-yeh-bee-l*eer* mee-yeem
It's for a present	**Hediye olarak** heh-dee-y*eh* oh-lah-r*ah*k
These are the measurements [*show written*]	**İşte ölçüleri** eesh-t*eh* erl-chooh-leh-r*ee*
bust	**büst** boohst
chest	**göğüs** gher-*oo*hs
collar	**yaka** yah-k*ah*
hip	**kalça** kahl-ch*ah*
leg	**bacak** bah-j*ah*k
waist	**bel** behl
Have you got something . . .	**. . . bir şeyiniz var mı?** beer sheh-yee-n*eez* vahr muh
in black?	**Siyah** see-y*ah*
in grey?	**Gri** gree
in blue?	**Mavi** mah-v*ee*
in brown?	**Kahverengi** kah-veh-rehn-ghee
in pink?	**Pembe** pehm-b*eh*
in green?	**Yeşil** yeh-sh*ee*l
in red?	**Kırmızı** kuhr-muh-z*uh*

in yellow?	**Sarı**
	sah-ru*h*
in this colour?	**Bu renkte**
	boo rehnk-teh
in cotton?	**Pamuklu**
	pah-mook-l*oo*
in denim?	**Blucin kumaşı**
	bloo-j*een* koo-mah-sh*uh*
in leather?	**Deri**
	deh-r*ee*
in nylon?	**Naylon**
	nay-l*ohn*
in suede?	**Süet**
	sooh-*eht*
in wool?	**Yünlü**
	yoohn-l*ooh*
in this material?	**Bu kumaştan**
	boo koo-mahsh-t*ahn*

[*For other essential expressions, see 'Shop talk', p. 50*]

Replacing equipment

ESSENTIAL INFORMATION

- Look for these shop signs:
  ELEKTRİKÇİ (electrician)
  HIRDAVATÇI (ironmonger)
  NALBUR (ironmonger)
  SÜPERMARKET (supermarket)
- To ask the way to the shop, see p. 17.

WHAT TO SAY

Have you got . . .	. . . var mı?
	vahr muh
an adaptor? [*show appliance*]	**Bir adaptör**
	beer ah-dahp-ter

a bottle of butane gas?	**Bir tüp bütan gazı**
	beer toop booh-tahn gah-zuh
a bottle opener?	**Bir şişe açacağı**
	beer shee-sheh ah-chah-jah-uh
a corkscrew?	**Bir tirbuşon**
	beer teer-boo-shohn
any disinfectant?	**Dezenfektan**
	deh-zehn-fehk-tahn
any paper/plastic cups?	**Kâğıt/plastik fincan**
	kah-uht/plahs-teek feen-jahn
any paper/plastic plates?	**Kâğıt/plastik tabak**
	kah-uht/plahs-teek tah-bahk
a drying-up cloth?	**Bir kurulama bezi**
	beer koo-roo-lah-mah beh-zee
any forks	**Çatallar**
	chah-tahl-lahr
a fuse? [*show an old one*]	**Bir sigorta**
	beer see-gohr-tah
an insecticide spray?	**Böcek öldürücüsü**
	ber-jehk erl-dooh-rooh-jooh-sooh
a kitchen roll? [*paper*]	**Mutfak kâğıdı**
	moot-fahk kah-uh-duh
any knives?	**Bıçaklar**
	buh-cahk-lahr
a light bulb [*show old one*]	**Bir ampul**
	beer ahm-pool
a plastic bucket?	**Bir plastik kova**
	beer plahs-teek koh-vah
a plug (for the sink)?	**Bir tıkaç (eviye için)**
	beer tuh-kahch (eh-vee-yeh ee-cheen)
a spanner?	**Bir anahtar**
	beer ah-nah-tahr
a sponge?	**Bir sünger**
	beer soohn-ghehr
any string?	**İp**
	eep
any tent pegs?	**Çadır kazığı**
	chah-duhr kah-zuh-uh
a tin opener?	**Konserve açacağı**
	kohn-sehr-veh ah-chah-jah-uh
a torch?	**Bir elfeneri**
	beer ehl-feh-neh-ree

any (torch) batteries?	**Pil (elfeneri için)**
	peel (ehl-feh-neh-*ree* ee-ch*ee*n)
a washing line?	**Bir çamaşır ipi**
	beer chah-mah-sh*u*hr ee-p*ee*
any washing powder?	**Çamaşır tozu**
	chah-mah-sh*u*hr toh-z*oo*
a washing-up brush?	**Bir bulaşık fırçası**
	beer boo-lah-sh*u*hk fuhr-chah-s*u*h
any washing-up liquid?	**Bulaşık deterjanı**
	boo-lah-sh*u*hk deh-tehr-jah-n*u*h

[*For other essential expressions, see 'Shop talk', below*]

Shop talk

ESSENTIAL INFORMATION

Know your coins and notes:
coins: 25, 50, 100 Turkish lira (TL)
notes: 100, 500, 1,000, 5,000, 10,000, 20,000.
● Know how to say the important weights and measures:

50 grams	**Elli gram**
	ehl-*lee* grahm
100 grams	**Yüz gram**
	yoohz gram
200 grams	**İki yüz gram**
	ee-k*ee* yoohz grahm
½ kilo	**Yarım kilo**
	yah-r*u*hm kee-loh
1 kilo	**Bir kilo**
	beer kee-loh
2 kilos	**İki kilo**
	ee-k*ee* kee-loh
½ litre	**Yarım litre**
	yah-r*u*hm lee-treh
1 litre	**Bir litre**
	beer lee-treh
2 litres	**İki litre**
	ee-k*ee* lee-treh

[*For numbers, see p. 118*]

CUSTOMER

Hello	**Merhaba**
	mehr-hah-bah
Good morning	**Günaydın**
	gooh-nay-duhn
Good day	**İyi günler**
	ee-yee goohn-lehr
Goodbye [*person staying*]	**Güle güle**
	gooh-leh gooh-leh
Goodbye [*person leaving*]	**Allahaısmarladık**
	ahl-lahs-mahr-lah-duhk
I'm just looking	**Sadece bakıyorum**
	sah-deh-jeh bah-kuh-yoh-room
Excuse me	**Affedersiniz**
	ahf-feh-dehr-see-neez
How much is this/that?	**Bu/şu ne kadar?**
	boo/shoo neh kah-dahr
What's that?	**Şu ne?**
	shoo neh
What are those?	**Şunlar ne?**
	shoon-lahr neh
Is there a discount?	**İskonto var mı?**
	ees-kohn-toh vahr muh
I'd like that, please	**Şunu istiyorum, lütfen**
	shoo-noo ees-tee-yoh-room looht-fehn
Not that	**Şunu değil**
	shoo-noo deh-eel
Like that	**Şunun gibi**
	shoo-noon gee-bee
That's enough, thank you	**O kadar yeter, teşekkür ederim**
	oh kah-dahr yeh-tehr teh-shehk-koohr eh-deh-reem
More, please	**Daha, lütfen**
	dah-hah looht-fehn
Less than that	**Ondan daha az**
	ohn-dahn dah-hah ahz
That's fine ⎤ OK ⎦	**Tamam**
	tah-mahm
I won't take it, thank you	**Almıyorum, teşekkür ederim**
	ahl-muh-yoh-room teh-shehk-koohr eh-deh-reem

It's not right	**Doğru değil** doh-r*oo* deh-*ee*l
Thank you very much	**Çok teşekkür ederim** chohk teh-shehk-k*oo*hr eh-deh-r*ee*m
Is there something . . .	**. . . bir şey var mı?** beer shehy vahr muh
better?	**Daha iyi** dah-h*ah* ee-y*ee*
cheaper?	**Daha ucuz** dah-h*ah* oo-j*oo*z
different?	**Başka** bahsh-k*ah*
larger?	**Daha büyük** dah-h*ah* booh-y*oo*hk
smaller?	**Daha küçük** dah-hah kooh-ch*oo*hk
At what time . . .	**Saat kaçta . . .** sah-*ah*t kahch-t*ah*
do you open?	**açıyor sunuz?** ah-ch*uh*-yohr soo-n*oo*z
do you close?	**kapatıyor sunuz?** kah-pah-t*uh*-yohr soo-n*oo*z
Can I have a bag, please?	**Bir çanta veriniz, lütfen** beer ch*ah*n-tah veh-ree-n*ee*z looht-fehn
Can I have a receipt?	**Bir makbuz veriniz** beer mahk-b*oo*z veh-ree-n*ee*z
Do you take . . .	**. . . alır mısınız?** ah-l*uh*r muh-suh-n*uh*z
English/American money?	**İngiliz/Amerikan parası** een-ghee-l*ee*z/ah-meh-ree-k*ah*n pah-rah-s*uh*
travellers' cheques?	**Seyahat çeki** seh-yah-h*ah*t cheh-k*ee*
credit cards?	**Kredi kartı** kreh-d*ee* kahr-t*uh*
I'd like . . .	**. . . istiyorum** ees-t*ee*-yoh-room
one like that	**Bir tane bunun gibi** beer tah-neh boo-n*oon* gee-b*ee*
two like that	**İki tane bunun gibi** ee-kee tah-neh boo-n*oon* gee-b*ee*

SHOP CLERK

Can I help you?	**Size yardım edebilir miyim?** see-zeh yahr-duhm eh-deh-bee-leer mee-yeem
What would you like?	**Ne istersiniz?** neh ees-tehr-see-neez
Will that be all?	**Başka bir şey var mı?** bahsh-kah beer shehy vahr muh
Would you like anything else?	**Başka bir şey ister misiniz?** bahsh-kah beer shehy ees-tehr mee-see-neez
Would you like it wrapped?	**Paket yapılım mı?** pah-keht yah-puh-luhm muh
Sorry, none left	**Özür dilerim, kalmadı** er-zoohr dee-leh-reem kahl-mah-duh
I haven't got any	**Yok** yohk
How many do you want?	**Kaç tane istersiniz?** kahch tah-neh ees-tehr-see-neez
Is that enough?	**Bu kadar yeter mi?** boo kah-dahr yeh-tehr mee

Shopping for food

Bread

ESSENTIAL INFORMATION

- For finding a baker's, see p. 17.
- Key words to look for:
  EKMEK (bread)
  EKMEKÇİ (baker)
  FIRIN (bakery)

- Bread is the staple food in Turkey and there are numerous bakeries everywhere. They open early in the morning and stay open till late at night. Supermarket, delicatessens and grocery stores also sell bread.
- Bread is sold by weight, the standard loaf being 1 kg. However, one normally asks for a certain number of loaves rather than a certain weight. Note that '**ekmek**' in Turkish means both 'bread' and 'loaf'. You can buy just half a loaf if you want only a small amount.

WHAT TO SAY

Some bread, please	**Ekmek, lütfen** ehk-mehk looht-fehn
One loaf (like that)	**Bir ekmek (şundan)** beer ehk-mehk (shoon-dahn)
A loaf	**Bir ekmek** beer ehk-mehk
Half a loaf	**Yarım ekmek** yah-ruhm ehk-mehk
A wholewheat loaf	**Bir kepek ekmeği** beer keh-pehk ehk-meh-*ee*
A French-style loaf	**Bir uzun ekmek** beer oo-zoon ehk-mehk
A 'milk' loaf [*made from dough to which milk is added*]	**Bir sütlü ekmek** beer sooht-looh ehk-mehk
A crescent-shaped loaf	**Bir ay** beer ay
A loaf of rye bread	**Bir çavdar ekmeği** beer chahv-dahr ehk-meh-*ee*
A bread roll	**Bir sandviç ekmeği** beer sahnd-veech ehk-meh-*ee*
Some sliced bread	**Tost ekmeği** tohst ehk-meh-*ee*
Two loaves	**İki ekmek** ee-kee ehk-mehk
Four bread rolls	**Dört sandviç ekmeği** derrt sahnd-veech ehk-meh-*ee*

[*For other essential expressions, see 'Shop talk', p. 50*]

Cakes, ice cream and sweets

ESSENTIAL INFORMATION

- Key words to look out for:
  BÖREKÇİ (pastry shop)
  DONDURMA (ice-cream)
  KURUYEMİŞÇİ (dried fruit, nut and sweet shop)
  MUHALLEBECİ (chicken, pudding, sweet and ice-cream shop)
  PASTANE (pastry and cake shop)
  ŞEKERLEME (confectionery)
  ŞEKERÇİ (confectionery shop)
- To find a cake shop etc., see p. 17.
- To order a snack, see p. 76.
- A vast range of pastries, cakes, puddings and sweets is available in Turkey. The list at the end of this section contains a selection of some of the best known.

WHAT TO SAY

Pastries and sweets are sold by weight, but with small items and slices of cakes and pastries you can always ask for them by portion, i.e. enough for one person, two people, etc.

100 grams of . . .	**Yüz gram . . .** yoohz grahm
200 grams of . . .	**İki yüz gram . . .** ee-kee yoohz grahm
½ kilo of . . .	**Yarım kilo . . .** yah-ruhm kee-loh
1 portion of . . .	**Bir porsiyon** beer pohr-see-yohn
2 portions of . . .	**İki porsiyon** ee-kee pohr-see-yohn
5 portions of . . .	**Beş porsiyon . . .** behsh pohr-see-yohn
chocolate cake	**çikolatalı pasta** chee-koh-lah-tah-luh pahs-tah
apple tart	**elmalı torta** ehl-mah-luh tohr-tah

mixed fruit tart	**karışık torta**
	kah-ruh-sh*u*hk tohr-t*a*h
Turkish delight	**lokum**
	loh-k*oo*m
baklava [*see list below*]	**baklava**
	bahk-lah-v*a*h

Some pastries come in two versions, one savoury, made with salt, the other sweet, made with sugar. So you might be given a choice of:

with salt	**tuzlu**
	tooz-l*oo*
with sugar	**şekerli**
	sheh-kehr-l*ee*

The word for ice-cream is **dondurma**.

I'd like a(n) . . . ice-cream	**Bir . . . dondurma istiyorum**
	beer . . . dohn-door-m*e*h ees-t*ee*-yoh-room
apricot	**kayısılı**
	kah-yuh-suh-l*u*h
cherry	**vişneli**
	veesh-neh-l*ee*
chocolate	**çikolatalı**
	chee-koh-lah-tah-l*u*h
lemon	**limonlu**
	lee-mohn-l*oo*
pistachio	**fıstıklı**
	fuhs-tuk-l*u*h
strawberry	**çilekli**
	ch*ee*-lehk-l*ee*
vanilla	**vanilyalı**
	vah-neel-yah-l*u*h
An ice-cream with whipped cream	**Bir şantiyeli dondurma**
	beer shahn-tee-yeh-l*ee* dohn-door-m*a*h
A chocolate-coated ice on a stick	**Bir panda**
	beer p*a*hn-dah
A packet of . . .	**Bir paket . . .**
	beer pah-k*e*ht

chocolates	**çikolata**
	chee-koh-l*a*h-tah
pistachio nuts	**fıstık**
	fuhs-t*u*hk

You may also like to try the following:

aşure
ah-sh*oo*-reh
pudding made from wheat, walnuts, raisins, figs etc.

baklava
bahk-lah-v*ah*
layered pastry stuffed with nuts and/or cream, steeped in syrup

badem kurabiyesi
bah-d*e*hm koo-rah-bee-yeh-s*ee*
almond cake

bülbül yuvası
b*oo*hl-b*oo*hl yoo-vah-s*uh*
'nightingale's nest': pastry in the shape of a nest, stuffed with walnuts

dilber dudağı
deel-b*e*hr doo-dah-*u*h
'beloved's lips': sponge and syrup pudding in the shape of lips

güllaç
goohl-l*a*hch
layered pastry with almonds cooked in milk

hanım göbeği
hah-n*u*hm gher-beh-*ee*
'lady's navel': sponge with hole in the middle, steeped in syrup

hanım parmağı
hah-n*u*hm pahr-mah-*u*h
'lady's finger': sponge fingers in syrup

helva
hehl-v*ah*
halva: crumbly cake of chopped nuts, honey and sesame seeds

kabak tatlısı
kah-b*ah*k taht-luh-s*uh*
sweet pumpkin sprinkled with chopped walnuts

kadayıf
kah-dah-y*uh*f
shredded wheat with nuts and syrup

keşkül-ü fırkara
kehsh-k*oo*hl-ooh fuhr-kah-r*ah*
milk pudding with almonds or pistachios

lokma
lohk-m*ah*
doughnut in syrup

lokum
loh-k*oo*m
Turkish delight: comes in a variety of flavours, with or without nuts

muhallebi
moo-hahl-leh-b*ee*
milk pudding

pelte
pehl-t*eh*
jelly

sarığı burma
sah-ruh-*uh* boor-m*ah*
'twisted turban': baklava in shape of a turban

sütlaç
sooht-*la*hch

rice pudding

tavuk göğsü
tah-w*oo*k gher-s*oo*h

blancmange-like milk pudding
   made with pounded chicken
   breast sprinkled with cinnamon

tulumba tatlısı
too-loom-b*a*h taht-luh-s*u*h

semolina doughsticks in syrup

vezir parmağı
veh-*zeer* pahr-mah-*u*h

'vizier's finger': sponge finger in
   syrup

zerde
zehr-d*e*h

sweet rice with saffron

At the supermarket

ESSENTIAL INFORMATION

- The signs to look out for are:
  ANKARA PAZARI
  MİGROS   supermarket chains
  SÜPERMARKET
- Supermarkets are a relatively new phenomenon in Turkey and
  none of them is very large. However, they are gradually becoming
  more common in the larger cities and resorts. The words in this
  section should also be useful in ordinary grocery stores
  (**BAKKAL**).
- For non-food items, see 'Replacing equipment', p. 48.
- No need to say anything in a supermarket, but ask if you can't
  find what you want.

WHAT TO SAY

Excuse me, please

Affedersiniz
ahf-feh-dehr-see-n*eez*

Where is . . .

. . . nerede?
neh-reh-d*e*h

the bread?

Ekmek
ehk-m*e*hk

the butter?	**Tereyağı** teh-reh-yah-*uh*
the cheese?	**Peynir** pehy-n*eer*
the chocolate?	**Çikolata** chee-koh-l*ah*-tah
the coffee?	**Kahve** kah-v*eh*
the cooking oil?	**Sıvı yağ** suh-v*uh* yah
the frozen food?	**Dondurulmuş yiyecekler** dohn-doo-rool-m*oo*sh yee-yeh- jehk-l*eh*r
the fruit?	**Meyva** mehy-v*ah*
the fruit juice?	**Meyva suyu** mehy-v*ah* soo-y*oo*
the jam?	**Reçel** reh-ch*eh*l
the meat?	**Et** eht
the milk?	**Süt** sooht
the mineral water?	**Maden suyu** mah-d*eh*n soo-y*oo*
the pasta?	**Makarna** mah-k*ah*r-nah
the salt?	**Tuz** tooz
the sugar?	**Şeker** sheh-k*eh*r
the tea?	**Çay** chay
the tinned fish?	**Konserve balık** kohn-s*eh*r-veh bah-l*uh*k
the tinned fruit?	**Konserve meyva** kohn-s*eh*r-veh mehy-v*ah*
the vegetables?	**Sebze** sehb-z*eh*
the vinegar?	**Sirke** seer-k*eh*
the wine?	**Şarap** shah-r*ah*p

the yogurt?	**Yoğurt**
	yoh-*oo*rt
Where are . . .	**. . . nerede?**
	neh-reh-d*e*h
the biscuits?	**Bisküvitler**
	bee-skooh-veet-l*e*hr
crisps?	**Cips**
	jeeps
the eggs?	**Yumurta**
	yoo-moor-t*a*h
the seafoods?	**Deniz ürünleri**
	deh-n*ee*z ooh-roohn-leh-r*ee*
the soft drinks?	**Meşrubat**
	mehsh-roo-b*a*ht
the sweets?	**Tatlılar**
	taht-luh-l*a*hr
the tinned vegetables?	**Konserve sebze**
	kohn-s*e*hr-veh sehb-z*e*h

[*For other essential expressions, see 'Shop talk', p. 50*]

Picnic food

ESSENTIAL INFORMATION

- Key words to look for:
  BAKKAL (grocer)
  ŞARKÜTERİ (delicatessen)
- Weight guide:
  4–6oz/150g of prepared salad per two people, if eaten as a starter to a substantial meal.
  3–4oz/100g of prepared salad per person, if to be eaten as the main part of a picnic-type meal.
- Since Turkey is predominantly a Muslim country, pork products are not easy to find.
- Chicken roasted on the spit can be bought to take away at many small restaurants. Look out for the sign **PAKET SERVİSİ** (take-away service).

WHAT TO SAY

One slice of . . .	**Bir dilim** . . .
	beer dee-l*ee*m
Two slices of . . .	**İki dilim** . . .
	ee-k*ee* dee-l*ee*m
roast beef	**rozbif**
	rohz-b*ee*f
tongue	**dil**
	deel
ham	**jambon**
	jahm-b*oh*n
garlic sausage	**sucuk**
	soo-j*oo*k
salami	**salam**
	sah-l*ah*m
100 grams of . . .	**Yüz gram** . . .
	yoohz grahm
150 grams of . . .	**Yüz elli gram** . . .
	yoohz ehl-l*ee* grahm
200 grams of . . .	**İki yüz gram** . . .
	ee-k*ee* yoohz grahm
300 grams of . . .	**Üç yüz gram** . . .
	oohch yoohz grahm
Russian salad	**Rus salatası**
	roos sah-lah-tah-s*u*h
tomato salad	**domates salatası**
	doh-m*ah*-tehs sah-lah-tah-s*u*h
beetroot salad	**pancar salatası**
	pahn-j*ah*r sah-lah-tah-s*u*h
carrot salad	**havuç salatası**
	hah-v*oo*ch sah-lah-tah-s*u*h
green salad	**yeşil salata**
	yeh-sh*ee*l sah-lah-tah
olives	**zeytin**
	zehy-t*ee*n
anchovies	**ançüvez**
	ahn-ch*oo*h-vehz
cheese	**peynir**
	pehy-n*ee*r
A (pot of) mayonnaise	**Bir mayonez**
	beer mah-yoh-n*e*hz

| A (pot of) mustard | **Bir hardal** |
| | beer hahr-dahl |

You might also like to try some of these:

acılı	cracked wheat,* tomato, parsley
ah-juh-luh	and hot pepper salad
cacık	yogurt and cucumber salad
jah-juhk	
haydari	cheese and yogurt dip
hay-dah-ree	
midye salatası	mussel salad
meed-yeh sah-lah-tah-suh	
pastırma	pastrami, spiced dried beef
pahs-tuhr-mah	
yaprak dolması	stuffed vine leaves
yah-prahk dohl-mah-suh	

These are the most commonly available cheeses:

beyaz peynir	white cheese, made from sheep's
beh-yahz pehy-neer	milk, like Greek feta cheese
Çerkez peyniri	a mild soft unsalted cheese
chehr-kehz pehy-nee-ree	
dil peyniri	a mild cheddar-like cheese
deel pehy-nee-ree	
gravyer	a gruyère-type cheese
grahv-yehr	
kaşer	a cheddar-like cheese
kah-shehr	
tulum peyniri	a hard salty cheese in a rind
too-loom pehy-nee-ree	

*Also known as burghul or bulgur.

Fruit and vegetables

ESSENTIAL INFORMATION

- Key words to look for:
  MEYVA/MEYVE (fruit)
  SEBZELER (vegetables)
  MANAV (greengrocer)
- If possible, buy fruit and vegetables in the market, where they are cheaper than in the shops.
- A kilo is roughly equivalent to 2lbs.

WHAT TO SAY

½ kilo of . . .	**Yarım kilo . . .**
	yah-r*u*hm kee-l*o*h
1 kilo of . . .	**Bir kilo . . .**
	beer kee-l*o*h
2 kilos of . . .	**İki kilo . . .**
	ee-k*ee* kee-l*o*h
apples	**elma**
	ehl-m*a*h
bananas	**muz**
	mooz
cherries	**kiraz**
	kee-r*a*hz
grapes	**üzüm**
	ooh-z*oo*hm
oranges	**portakal**
	pohr-tah-k*a*hl
pears	**armut**
	ahr-m*oo*t
peaches	**şeftali**
	shehf-t*a*h-lee
plums	**erik**
	eh-r*ee*k
strawberries	**çilek**
	chee-l*e*hk
A pineapple, please	**Bir ananas, lütfen**
	beer ah-nah-n*a*hs l*oo*ht-fehn

A grapefruit	**Bir greyfrut**
	beer grehy-fr*oo*t
A melon	**Bir kavun**
	beer kah-w*oo*n
A water melon	**Bir karpuz**
	beer kahr-p*oo*z
1 kilo of . . .	**Bir kilo . . .**
	beer kee-l*o*h
artichokes	**enginar**
	ehn-ghee-n*a*hr
aubergines	**patlıcan**
	paht-luh-j*a*hn
carrots	**havuç**
	hah-w*oo*ch
courgettes	**kabak**
	kah-b*a*hk
green beans	**yeşil fasulye**
	yeh-sh*ee*l fah-s*oo*l-yeh
leeks	**pırasa**
	puh-r*a*h-sah
mushrooms	**mantar**
	mahn-t*a*hr
onions	**soğan**
	soh-*a*hn
peas	**bezelye**
	beh-zehl-y*e*h
potatoes	**patates**
	pah-t*a*h-tehs
red cabbage	**kırmızı lahana**
	kuhr-muh-z*u*h l*a*h-hah-nah
spinach	**ıspanak**
	uhs-pah-n*a*hk
tomatoes	**domates**
	doh-m*a*h-tes
A bunch of parsley	**Bir demet maydanoz**
	beer deh-m*e*ht may-dah-n*o*hz
A bunch of radishes	**Bir demet turp**
	beer deh-m*e*ht toorp
A head of garlic	**Bir baş sarmısak**
	beer bahsh sahr-muh-s*a*hk
A lettuce	**Bir salata**
	beer sah-l*a*h-tah

A cauliflower	**Bir karnabahar**
	beer kahr-nah-bah-h*a*r
A cabbage	**Bir lahana**
	beer l*a*h-hah-nah
A cucumber	**Bir salatalık**
	beer sah-lah-tah-l*u*hk
Like that, please	**Bundan, lütfen**
	boon-d*a*hn l*oo*ht-fehn

You might also like to try these:

kabak	pumpkin
kah-b*a*hk	
kereviz	celery root
keh-reh-v*ee*z	
nar	pomegranate
nahr	
ayva	quince
ay-v*a*h	

[*For other essential information, see 'Shop talk', p. 50*]

Meat

ESSENTIAL INFORMATION

- Key words to look out for:
  KASAP (butcher)
  CİĞERCİ (offal shop)
- Weight guide: 4–6oz/125–200g of meat per person for one meal.
- A wide range of cuts is available, though you may not find exactly the same ones as at home. If in doubt, tell the butcher whether you intend to stew, grill or roast the meat, so that he will know what to give you.
- Offal is very popular in Turkey and a full range is available in special shops called **CİĞERCİ**.
- If you want the best-quality mince, choose a piece of meat and ask the butcher to mince it for you.

- Mutton tends to have a stronger flavour than most English palates are nowadays accustomed to.
- Turkey is predominantly a Muslim country, so pork (**domuz**) is very difficult to find.

WHAT TO SAY

For a joint, choose the type of meat you want and then say how many people it is for and how you intend to cook it.

Some beef, please	**Sığır, lütfen** suh-uhr looht-fehn
Some lamb	**Kuzu** koo-zoo
Some mutton	**Koyun** koh-yoon
Some veal	**Dana** dah-nah
A joint . . .	**Rostoluk et . . .** rohs-toh-look eht
Meat for shish kebabs . . .	**Şişlik et . . .** sheesh-leek eht
for two people	**iki kişi için** ee-kee kee-shee ee-cheen
for four people	**dört kişi için** derrt kee-shee ee-cheen
for six people	**altı kişi için** ahl-tuh kee-shee ee-cheen
I want . . . the meat	**Eti . . . istiyorum** eh-tee . . . ees-tee-yoh-room
to boil	**haşlamalık** hahsh-lah-mah-luhk
to grill	**ızgaralık** uhz-gah-rah-luhk
to roast	**kavurmalık** kah-voor-mah-luhk

For steak, liver or kidneys, do as above.

Some steak, please	**Biftek, lütfen** beef-tehk looht-fehn

Sirloin steak	**Bonfile** bohn-fee-leh
Some liver	**Ciğer** jee-ehr
Some kidneys	**Böbrek** ber-brehk
for three people	**üç kişi için** oohch kee-shee ee-cheen
for five people	**beş kişi için** behsh kee-shee ee-cheen

For chops, do it this way:

Two veal escalopes, please	**İki dana eskalop, lütfen** ee-kee dah-nah ehs-kah-lohp looht-fehn
Five lamb chops	**Beş kuzu pirzolası** behsh koo-zoo peer-zoh-lah-suh

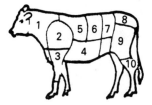

Beef and veal
Sığır ve dana

1 **Gerdan**
2 **Kürek**
3 **Kol**
4 **Göğüs; döş**
5 **Pirzola**
6 **File**
7 **Antrekotlet**
8 **Sokum**
9 **Tranş; nua**
10 **Bacak**

Lamb and mutton
Kuzu ve koyun

1 **Kol**
2 **Kürek**
3 **Pirzola**
4 **Fileto**
5 **Göğüs**
6 **But**

You may also want:

A chicken	**Piliç**
	pee-*lee*ch
A duck	**Ördek**
	err-d*e*hk
Quail	**Bıldırcın**
	buhl-duhr-j*u*hn
A rabbit	**Tavşan**
	tahv-sh*a*hn
Some tongue	**Dil**
	deel

Other essential expressions (*see also p. 50*):

Please . . .	**Lütfen . . .**
	l*oo*ht-fehn
mince it	**kıyınız**
	kuh-yuh-n*uh*z
dice it	**kuşbaşı**
	koosh-bah-sh*uh*
trim the fat	**yağını çıkartınız**
	yah-uh-n*uh* chuh-kahr-tuh-n*uh*z

Fish

ESSENTIAL INFORMATION

- Look out for:
  BALIKÇI (fishmonger)
- Fish can also be bought in fish markets and, in ports, on the quay
  where the fishing boats come in.

- Weight guide: 8oz/250g minimum per person for one meal of fish bought on the bone.

  i.e. ½ kilo/500g   for two people
      1 kilo   for four people
      1½ kilo   for six people

- It is not normal practice in Turkey for the fishmonger to fillet fish, and you may also find that some fishmongers will not clean fish – so bear this in mind when choosing what to buy.
- A wide range of excellent fresh fish is available in the coastal regions, according of course to season. Some types of fish will be unfamiliar but well worth trying, as many are delicious.

WHAT TO SAY

Fish is bought by the kilo or, with larger fish and some shellfish, it can also be bought by the item ('**tane**' in Turkish).
[*For numbers, see p. 118*]

½ kilo of	**Yarım kilo . . .** yah-r*u*hm kee-l*o*h
1 kilo of . . .	**Bir kilo . . .** beer kee-l*o*h
1½ kilo of . . .	**Bir buçuk kilo . . .** beer boo-ch*oo*k kee-loh
One . . .	**Bir tane . . .** beer tah-n*e*h
Two . . .	**İki tane . . .** ee-k*ee* tah-n*e*h
Three . . .	**Üç tane . . .** oohch tah-n*e*h
anchovy	**hamsi** hahm-s*ee*
bass	**levrek** lehv-r*e*hk
blue fish	**lüfer** looh-f*e*hr
bonito	**palamut** pah-lah-m*oo*t
bream	**karagöz** kah-rah-g*e*rz
brill	**pisi** pee-s*ee*

cod	**bakalyaro/mezgit**
	bah-kahl-yah-roh/mehz-geet
eel	**yılan balığı**
	yuh-lahn bah-luh-uh
gar fish	**zargana**
	zahr-gah-nah
gilt-head bream	**çipura**
	chee-poo-rah
goby	**kaya balığı**
	kah-yah bah-luh-uh
mackerel	**uskumru/kolyoz/istavrit**
	oos-koom-roo/kohl-yohz/ees-tah-vreet
mullet (grey)	**kefal**
	keh-fahl
mullet (red, small)	**tekir**
	teh-keer
mullet (red)	**barbunya**
	bahr-boon-yah
octopus	**ahtapod**
	ah-tah-pohd
pandora	**mercan**
	mehr-jahn
sandsmelt	**gümüş**
	gooh-moohsh
sardine	**sardalya**
	sahr-dahl-yah
scorpion fish	**iskorpit**
	ees-kohr-peet
squid	**kalamar**
	kah-lah-mahr
sole	**dil**
	deel
sturgeon	**mersin balığı**
	mehr-seen bah-luh-uh
swordfish	**kılıç balığı**
	kuh-luhch bah-luh-uh
tub fish	**kırlangıç balığı**
	kuhr-lahn-guhch bah-luh-uh
turbot	**kalkan**
	kahl-kahn
whiting	**mezgit/bakalyaro**
	mehz-geet/bah-kahl-yah-roh

Some large fish can be purchased by the slice:

One slice of . . .	**Bir dilim . . .**
	beer dee-l*ee*m
Two slices of . . .	**İki dilim . . .**
	ee-k*ee* dee-l*ee*m
Six slices of . . .	**Altı dilim . . .**
	ahl-t*uh* dee-l*ee*m
cod	**bakalyaro**
	bah-kahl-y*a*h-roh
tuna	**ton**
	tohn
turbot	**kalkan**
	kahl-k*a*hn

Shellfish

Crab	**Yengeç/pavurya**
	yehn-gh*e*hch/pah-v*oo*r-yah
Mussels	**Midye**
	m*ee*d-yeh
Oysters	**İstiridye**
	ees-tee-r*ee*d-yeh
Prawns	**Karides**
	kah-r*ee*-dehs
Scallops	**Tarak**
	tah-r*a*hk
Shrimp	**Kerevet**
	keh-reh-v*e*ht

Other essential expressions (*see also p. 50*):

Please . . .	**Lütfen . . .**
	l*oo*ht-fehn
take the head off	**kafayı çıkartınız**
	kah-fah-y*uh* chuh-kahr-tuh-n*uh*z
clean them	**temizleyiniz**
	teh-meez-leh-yee-n*ee*z

Eating and drinking out

Ordering a drink

ESSENTIAL INFORMATION

- Key words to look for:
  BAR
  BİRHANE (beer hall/pub)
  BÜFE (snack bar)
  ÇAYHANE (tea house)
  KAFETERİA (cafeteria)
  MEYHANE (tavern)
- Except in places where drinks are consumed standing at a counter, there is nearly always waiter service and one should leave a tip.
- Excellent fruit juices made from freshly pressed fruit are very popular in Turkey. Look for the sign **MEYVA SUYU** (fruit juice).
- Tea is the national hot drink in Turkey. It is served, without milk, in small glasses. During the summer there are many pleasant tea gardens (**ÇAY BAHÇESİ**) where people go to relax with their families and friends.
- The national alcoholic drink is **rakı**. This aniseed-flavoured grape spirit, which closely resembles Middle Eastern arak and Greek ouzo, is usually mixed with water and/or ice. **Rakı** is drunk both on its own and as an accompaniment to food.
- There are also locally produced gin and vodka, which are very much cheaper than imported brands, and a variety of Turkish wines, some of which are very drinkable.
- Bottled beer of the lager type is good quality and widely available. Some pubs and taverns serve draft lager – look out for the sign **FIÇI BİRA** (barrel beer).
- The **kahve**, or old-style Turkish coffee house, is an exclusively male preserve where the men go to talk, do business and play cards and backgammon. Tea and coffee, but not alcoholic drinks, are served.
- When asking for Turkish coffee, one specifies how sweet one wants it (because the sugar is added while the water and coffee mixture is being heated).

WHAT TO SAY

I'd like . . .	**. . . istiyorum** ees-*tee*-yoh-room
a Turkish coffee	**bir Türk kahvesi** beer toohrk kah-veh-s*ee*
without sugar	**Sade** s*a*h-deh
with a little sugar	**Az şekerli** ahz sheh-kehr-l*ee*
medium sweet	**Orta şekerli** ohr-t*a*h sheh-kehr-l*ee*
sweet	**Şekerli** sheh-kehr-l*ee*
a (black) coffee	**bir neskafé** beer nehs-kah-feh
with milk	**Sütlü** sooht-l*oo*h
a tea	**bir çay** beer ch*a*y
with milk	**Sütlü** sooht-l*oo*h
with lemon	**Limonlu** lee-mohn-l*oo*
a glass of milk	**Bir süt** beer sooht
two glasses of milk	**İki süt** ee-k*ee* sooht
a drinking chocolate	**Bir sütlü kakao** beer sooht-l*oo*h kah-kah-*oh*
a mineral water	**Bir maden suyu** beer mah-d*eh*n soo-y*oo*
a lemonade	**Bir limonata** beer lee-moh-n*a*h-tah
a lemon juice	**Bir limon suyu** beer lee-mohn soo-y*oo*
a Coca Cola	**Bir Koka Kola** beer k*oh*-kah k*oh*-lah
an orangeade	**Bir portakallı gazoz** beer pohr-tah-kahl-l*u*h gah-z*oh*z
an orange juice	**Bir portakal suyu** beer pohr-tah-k*a*hl soo-y*oo*

a grape juice	**Bir üzüm suyu**
	beer ooh-zoohm soo-yoo
a pineapple juice	**Bir ananas suyu**
	beer ah-nah-nahs soo-yoo
a small bottle of beer	**Küçük bir bira**
	kooh-choohk beer bee-rah
a large bottle of beer	**Büyük bir bira**
	booh-yoohk beer bee-rah
a draught beer	**bir fıçı birası**
	beer fuh-chuh bee-rah-suh
small	**Kücük**
	kooh-chook
large	**Büyük**
	booh-yoohk
a bottle of wine	**Bir şişe şarap**
	beer shee-sheh shah-rahp
a small bottle of wine	**Küçük bir şişe şarap**
	kooh-choohk beer shee-sheh shah-rahp
red	**kırmızı**
	kuhr-muh-zuh
white	**beyaz**
	beh-yahz
rosé	**roze**
	roh-zeh
dry	**sek**
	sehk
medium sweet	**demi sek**
	deh-mee sehk
sparkling	**köpüklü**
	ker-poohk-looh
A bottle of champagne	**Bir şişe şampanya**
	beer shee-sheh shahm-pahn-yah
A whisky	**Bir viski**
	beer vees-kee
with ice	**buz ile**
	booz ee-leh
with (mineral) water	**(maden) suyu ile**
	(mah-dehn) soo-yoo ee-leh
with soda	**soda ile**
	soh-dah ee-leh

A gin	**Bir cin**
	beer jeen
A gin and tonic	**Bir cin-tonik**
	beer jeen-toh-neek
with lemon	**limon ile**
	lee-mohn ee-leh
A vodka	**Bir votka**
	beer voht-kah
A vodka and tonic	**Bir votka-tonik**
	beer voht-kah-toh-neek
A brandy	**Bir konyak**
	beer kohn-yahk

You may also like to try these local beverages:

ayran	a yogurt drink (very slightly salty)
ay-rahn	served cold; very popular,
	especially in summer
boza	a winter drink made from
boh-zah	fermented millet sprinkled with
	cinnamon
salep	another winter drink made of hot
sah-lehp	milk flavoured with orchis root
	and sprinkled with cinnamon

Other essential expressions:

Waiter!	**Bakar mısınız!**
	bah-kahr muh-suh-nuhz
The bill, please	**Hesabı, lütfen**
	heh-sah-buh looht-fehn
How much?	**Ne kadar?**
	neh kah-dahr
Is service included?	**Servis dahil mi?**
	sehr-vees dah-heel mee
Where is the toilet, please?	**Tuvalet nerede, lütfen?**
	too-wah-leht neh-reh-deh looht-fehn

Ordering a snack

ESSENTIAL INFORMATION

- Look out for these signs:
  BAR
  BÖREKÇİ (pastry shop)
  BÜFE (snack bar)
  CAFE
  KAFETERİA (cafeteria)
- All the above places serve drinks as well as food (though some places serve only soft drinks).
- Look for the names of snacks in the windows.
- For cakes, ice-creams and sweets, see p. 55.
- For picnic-type snacks, see p. 60.
- Note that in Turkey a '**sandviç**' means a roll with a filling, rather than a 'sandwich'. However, toasted sandwiches – '**tost**' – are made with sliced bread.

WHAT TO SAY

I'd like . . .	. . . istiyorum
	ees-*tee*-yoh-room
a cheese roll	**Bir peynirli sandviç**
	beer pehy-neer-*lee* sahnd-v*ee*ch
an egg roll	**Bir yumurtalı sandviç**
	beer yoo-moor-tah-l*uh* sahnd-v*ee*ch
a hamburger	**Bir hamburger**
	beer hahm-boor-gh*e*hr
a hot dog	**Bir sosisli sandviç**
	beer soh-sees-*lee* sahnd-v*ee*ch
a toasted sandwich	**Bir tost**
	beer tohst
an ice-cream	**Bir dondurma**
	beer dohn-door-m*a*h
a bag of crisps	**Bir paket cips**
	beer pah-k*e*ht jeeps

You may also like to try the following:

börek ber-*rehk*	savoury pastries filled with cheese, minced meat, spinach etc.
lâhmacun lah-mah-*joon*	Turkish-style pizza: soft bread topped with minced meat, chopped tomatoes and red pepper, served hot
leblebi lehb-leh-b*ee*	roasted chickpeas, prepared in various ways, salted and unsalted, sold either by dried fruit shops (**KURUYEMİŞÇİ**) or street vendors
midye tava m*ee*d-yeh tah-v*ah*	mussels on sticks, deep-fried in batter, available from street vendors
simit see-m*eet*	bread rings covered in sesame seeds, sold by street vendors

[*For other essential expressions, see 'Ordering a drink', p. 72*]

At a restaurant

ESSENTIAL INFORMATION

- The place to ask for: **bir lokanta**
- You can eat at these places:
  BALIK LOKANTASI (fish restaurant)
  BÖREKÇİ (for savoury pastries)
  İSKEMBECİ (restaurant specializing in tripe soup)
  KEBABÇİ (kebab restaurant)
  KÖFTECİ (for grilled Turkish-style hamburger)
  LOKANTA (restaurant)
  MUHALLEBİCİ (restaurant specializing in chicken)
  PİDECİ (for Turkish-style pizzas)
  RESTORAN (restaurant)
- By law menus and prices must be displayed in the restaurant.

- In self-service restaurants you choose what you want from a display of hot and cold dishes and then, usually, your tray is brought by a waiter to your table.
- A service charge of 10% is generally included in the bill. However, it is customary to leave a further tip of about 5–10% (or even more – if you are pleased with the service).
- Eating times tend to be earlier than in other Mediterranean countries.
- Not all restaurants serve alcoholic drinks, so if you do want a drink with your meal check before you order.

WHAT TO SAY

May I book a table?	**Rezervasyon yapabilir miyim?** reh-zehr-vahs-yohn yah-pah-bee-leer mee-yeem
I've booked a table	**Rezervasyonum var** reh-zehr-vahs-yoh-noom vahr
A table . . .	**. . . masa** mah-sah
for one	**Bir kişilik** beer kee-shee-leek
for three	**Üç kişilik** oohch kee-shee-leek
The menu, please	**Mönüyü, lütfen** mer-nooh-yooh looht-fehn
The fixed-price menu	**Tabldot** tahbl-doh
The tourist menu	**Turistik mönüyü** too-rees-teek mer-nooh-yooh
Today's special menu	**Bugünkü mönüyü** boo-goohn-kooh mer-nooh-yooh
What's this, please?	**Bu ne, lütfen?** boo neh looht-fehn
Some wine, please	**Şarap, lütfen** shah-rahp looht-fehn
A bottle	**Bir şişe** beer shee-sheh
A half-bottle	**Yarım şişe** yah-ruhm shee-sheh
Red/white/rosé	**Kırmızı/beyaz/roze** kuhr-muh-zuh/beh-yahz/roh-zeh

Some beer	**Bira**
	bee-rah
Some more bread, please	**Biraz daha ekmek, lütfen**
	bee-rahz dah-hah ehk-mehk looht-fehn
Some more wine	**Daha şarap**
	dah-hah shah-rahp
Some oil	**Yağı**
	yah-uh
Some vinegar	**Sirke**
	seer-keh
Some salt	**Tuz**
	tooz
Some pepper	**Biber**
	bee-behr
Some mineral water	**Maden suyu**
	mah-dehn soo-yoo
How much does that come to?	**Borçum ne kadar?**
	bohr-choom neh kah-dahr
Is service included?	**Servis dahil mi?**
	sehr-vees dah-heel mee
Where is the toilet, please?	**Tuvalet nerede, lütfen?**
	too-wah-leht neh-reh-deh looht-fehn
Excuse me! [*when trying to get the waiter's attention*]	**Bakar mısınız!**
	bah-kahr muh-suh-nuhz
The bill, please	**Hesabı, lütfen**
	heh-sah-buh looht-fehn
May I have a receipt	**Bir makbuz veriniz**
	beer mahk-booz veh-ree-neez

Key words for courses as seen on some menus

[*Only ask this question if you want the waiter to remind you of the choice*]

What have you got in the way of . . .	**. . . olarak ne var?**
	oh-lah-rahk neh vahr
STARTERS?	**MEZE**
	meh-zeh
SOUP?	**ÇORBA**
	chohr-bah

EGG DISHES?	**YUMURTA**
	yoo-moor-*tah*
FISH?	**BALIK**
	bah-l*u*hk
MEAT?	**ET**
	eht
MAIN DISHES?	**ANA YEMEK**
	ah-n*ah* yeh-m*eh*k
GRILLS?	**IZGARA**
	uhz-gah-r*ah*
VEGETABLES?	**SEBZE**
	sehb-*zeh*
SALADS?	**SALATA**
	sah-l*ah*-tah
CHEESE?	**PEYNİR**
	pehy-n*ee*r
FRUIT?	**MEYVA**
	mehy-v*ah*
ICE-CREAM?	**DONDURMA**
	dohn-door-m*ah*
DESSERTS?	**TATLI**
	taht-l*u*h

UNDERSTANDING THE MENU

- You will find that some menus in Turkey are in one or more European languages. However, if in doubt ask to look at the different dishes – the staff will always be happy to show you.
- It is the custom in many places to bring a large tray of starters (**mezeler**) to the table from which you can choose the ones you want.
- If something is brought to the table that you do not want, do not hesitate to say so – it will not cause offence.
- You will find the names of the principal ingredients of most dishes on these pages:

  Starters, see p. 62   Fruit, see p. 63
  Meat, see p. 65   Dessert, see p. 57
  Fish, see p. 68   Cheese, see p. 62
  Vegetables, see p. 63   Ice-cream, see p. 55
- The following list of cooking and menu terms should help you to decode the menu.

Cooking and menu terms

Adana kebabı	hot, spicy minced meat kebab
acılı	salad of cracked wheat, tomato and chopped hot red peppers
ançüvez	anchovies
Arnavut ciğeri	'Albanian liver': spicy diced liver served with raw onions
ayva	quince
az pişmiş	rare
balık	fish
balık çorbası	fish soup
balık köftesi	fried fish cakes
bamya	okra, ladies' fingers
beyin ızgara	grilled lamb's brains
beyin salatası	lamb's brains with oil and lemon juice
bezelye	peas
beyaz peynir	white sheep's milk cheese, like Greek feta
biber dolması	stuffed green pepper
biftek	steak
bonfile	sirloin steak
böbrek ızgara	grilled kidneys
börek	pastry with various savoury fillings, baked or deep fried
buğulama	steamed, poached
bulgur	cracked wheat
Bursa kebabı	grilled lamb with pitta bread, tomato and yoghurt
cacık	yoghurt with chopped cucumber and garlic
ciğer	liver
Çerkez tavuğu	'Circassian chicken': chicken served with walnut and garlic sauce
çevirme	roasted on a spit
çiğ	raw
Çoban salatası	'shepherd's salad': chopped tomato, cucumber, green pepper, parsley and onions
çok pişmiş	well done

çorba	soup
çömlek kebabı	meat and vegetable stew
deniz ürünleri	seafood
dil	tongue, or sole
dil söğüş	cold sliced tongue
dolma	stuffed vegetables
domates	tomato
domates salatası	tomato salad
döner kebap	slices of grilled lamb cut from meat cooked on a vertical spit
düğün çorbası	'wedding soup': lamb broth cooked with eggs and lemon
ekmek	bread
enginar	artichokes
et	meat
etli	with meat
ezme	purée
fasulye	beans
fasulye pilâki	cold beans in olive oil
fasulye piyazi	beans and onions
fava	puréed beans
fırında	baked or roasted in the oven
günün çorbası	soup of the day
güveç	meat and vegetable casserole
hamsi	anchovies
haşlama	boiled, stewed
kaynamış yumurta	boiled egg
havuç	carrots
haydari	white cheese mashed in yoghurt with thyme
hıyar	cucumber
hünkar beğendi	'emperor's delight': roast lamb with puréed aubergine
ıspanak	spinach
ıspanaklı börek	pastry with a spinach filling
ızgara	grilled
iç pilav	rice with chopped liver and pine nuts
içki	alcoholic drink
içli köfte	spiced minced meat, fried in a cracked wheat casing

imam bayıldı	'the imam fainted': aubergine stuffed with onion and tomato, cooked in olive oil and served cold
İskender kebap	a mixture of different kinds of kebab meat (**döner**, **şiş** etc.)
islim kebabı	lamb and vegetable pie
iskembe çorbası	tripe soup
iyi pişmiş	well-done
kabak	courgettes, marrow, pumpkin
kabak dolması	stuffed courgettes (zucchini)
kadın budu köfte	'lady's thigh': fried meatballs
kağıt kebabı	lamb and vegetables baked in paper
kağıtta pişmiş	baked in paper
kalamar	squid
kara zeytin	black olives
karides güveç	prawn casserole, with tomatoes and cheese
karnabahar	cauliflower
karnıyarık	aubergine with meat filling
kereviz	celery root
kısır	cracked wheat with paprika
kıymalı	with minced meat
kıymalı börek	pastry with mincemeat filling
kıvırcık salata	curly-leaved lettuce
kızartma	fried
koç yumurtası	'ram's eggs': ram's testicles
kotlet	cutlet
koyun eti	mutton
köfte	meatball, hamburger
kuru fasulye	green beans with tomato sauce
kuzu dolması	roast lamb with rice
kuzu eti	lamb
kuzu fırında	roast lamb
kuzu pirzolası	lamb chops
lahana dolması	stuffed cabbage leaves
lakerda salatası	sliced salted bonito (fish) salad
limon	lemon
Macar gulaşı	Hungarian goulash
maden suyu	mineral water
makarna	macaroni, pasta
mantar	mushrooms

mantı	Turkish-style ravioli
marul	lettuce
maydanoz	parsley
menemen	tomato and pepper omelette
mercimek	lentils
meşrubat	soft drinks
mevsim salatası	salad of the season
meze	starter, hors-d'oeuvre
midye dolması	mussels in their shells stuffed with rice and pine nuts
midye tava	mussels deep-fried on a stick in batter
muska böreği	triangles of pastry with various different fillings
omlet	omelette
Orman kebap	lamb casserole with carrots, potatoes and tomatoes
orta pişmiş	medium (cooked)
ördek	duck
paça	sheep's trotters in sauce
pancar	beetroot
pane	with breadcrumbs
pastırma	dried cured beef, pastrami
patates/tava kızartması	chips, french fries
patlıcan	aubergine
patlıcan dolması	stuffed aubergine
patlıcan salatası	aubergine salad
peynirli	with cheese
pilâki	white kidney beans in olive oil
pilav	rice
piliç	chicken
piliç ızgarası	grilled chicken
pirzola	a chop
pişkin	well-done
piyaz	green bean salad
roka	rocket, green salad leaf
rosto	roasted
Rus salatası	Russian salad
sahanda yumurta	fried eggs
salatalık	cucumber
salçalı	with tomato sauce
salçalı köfte	meatballs in tomato sauce
sandviç ekmek	bread roll

sarmısak	garlic
sebze çorbası	vegetable soup
sıcak	hot
sığır eti	beef
sigara böreği	pastry rolled into a cigarette shape with cheese or minced meat filling
soğan	onion
soğuk	cold
sosis	frankfurter-type sausage
soslu	with sauce
su böreği	baked layers of pastry stuffed with cheese or meat
sucuk	Turkish garlic sausage
şehriye	vermicelli
şiş kebap	skewered pieces of charcoal-grilled lamb
şiş köfte	skewered ground lamb meatballs, grilled
tarama salatası	smoked cod's roe salad
tas kebap	stewed meat in tomato sauce
tava	fried
tavuk	chicken
tavuk çorbası	chicken soup
terbiyeli	with egg and lemon sauce
tereyağı	butter
turp	radish
turşu	pickled vegetables
tükenmez	fried eggs with tomato and peppers
türlü	meat and vegetable stew
uykuluk	sweetbreads
viyana şinitzel	Wiener schnitzel
yahni	meat stewed with onions
yaprak dolması	stuffed vine or cabbage leaves
yaprak sarması	stuffed vine or cabbage leaves
yayla çorbası	yoghurt soup
yeşil salata	green salad
yeşil zeytin	green olives
yoğurtlu	with yoghurt
yumurta	egg
yumurtalı	with egg
yürek ızgara	grilled heart
zeytin	olives
zeytinyağlı	with olive oil

Health

ESSENTIAL INFORMATION

- In Turkey there are both State and privately run medical services. Turkish nationals receive free treatment in State hospitals, but many people with the funds to do so opt for the private system. When visiting Turkey it is essential to have proper medical insurance. A policy can be bought through a travel agent, a broker or a motoring organization.
- Take your own 'first line' first aid kit with you.
- For minor disorders and treatment at a chemist's, see p. 37.
- For finding your way to a doctor, dentist and chemist, see p. 17.
- Once in Turkey, decide on a definite plan of action in case of serious illness: communicate your problem to a near neighbour, the receptionist or someone you see regularly. You are then dependent on that person helping you obtain treatment.
- In an emergency, say '**Doktor istiyorum**' (dohk-tohr ees-tee-yoh-room): 'I need a doctor' – and if necessary keep saying '**Doktor**' until you get some response.
- Also look out for these signs:
  AMBULANS (ambulance)
  DİŞÇİ (dentist)
  GÖZLÜKÇÜ (optician)
  HASTANE (hospital)
  İLKYARDIM HASTANESİ (first aid hospital)
  KLİNİK (clinic)
  MUAYENEHANE (surgery)

WHAT'S THE MATTER

I have a pain . . .	. . . ağrıyor
	ah-ruh-yohr
in my abdomen	**Karnım**
	kahr-nuhm
in my ankle	**Ayak bileğim**
	ah-yahk bee-leh-eem
in my arm	**Kolum**
	koh-loom
in my back	**Sırtım**
	suhr-tuhm

in my bladder	**Mesânem**
	meh-sah-nehm
in my bowels	**Barsaklarım**
	bahr-sahk-lah-ruhm
in my breast	**Göğsüm**
	gher-soohm
in my chest	**Göğsüm**
	gher-soohm
in my ear	**Kulağım**
	koo-lah-uhm
in my eye	**Gözüm**
	gher-zoohm
in my foot	**Ayağım**
	ah-yah-uhm
in my head	**Başım**
	bah-shuhm
in my heel	**Topuğum**
	toh-poo-oom
in my jaw	**Çene kemiğim**
	cheh-neh keh-mee-eem
in my kidneys	**Böbreğim**
	ber-breh-eem
in my leg	**Bacağım**
	bah-jah-uhm
in my lung	**Akciğerim**
	ahk-jee-eh-reem
in my neck	**Boynum**
	boy-noom
in my penis	**Penisim**
	peh-nee-seem
in my shoulder	**Omuzum**
	oh-moo-zoom
in my stomach	**Midem**
	mee-dehm
in my testicles	**Erbezlerim**
	ehr-behz-leh-reem
in my throat	**Boğazım**
	boh-ah-zuhm
in my vagina	**Vaginam**
	vah-ghee-nahm
in my wrist	**Bileğim**
	bee-leh-eem

I have a pain here [*point*]	**Buramda bir ağrı var**
	boo-rahm-d*a*h beer ah-r*u*h vahr
I have a toothache	**Dişim ağrıyor**
	dee-sh*ee*m ah-r*u*h-yohr
I have broken . . .	**. . . kırıldı**
	kuh-ruhl-d*u*h
my dentures	**Takma dişim**
	tahk-m*a*h dee-sh*ee*m
my glasses	**Gözlüğüm**
	gherz-looh-*oo*hm
I have lost my contact lens	**Kontakt lensimi kaybettim**
	kohn-t*a*hkt lehn-see-m*ee* kay-beht-t*ee*m
I have lost a filling	**Dolgum düştü**
	dohl-g*u*hm doohsh-t*oo*
My child is ill	**Çocuğum hasta**
	choh-joo-*oo*m hahs-t*a*h
He/she has a pain here [*point*]	**Burası ağrıyor**
	boo-rah-s*u*h ah-r*u*h-yohr

[*For parts of the body, see list above.*]

How bad is it?

I'm ill	**Hastayım**
	hah-stah-y*u*hm
It's urgent	**Acele**
	ah-jeh-l*e*h
It's serious	**Ağır**
	ah-*u*hr
It's not serious	**Önemi yok**
	er-neh-m*ee* yohk
It hurts	**Ağrıyor**
	ah-r*u*h-yohr
It hurts a lot	**Çok ağrıyor**
	chohk ah-r*u*h-yohr
It doesn't hurt much	**Çok ağrımıyor**
	chohk ah-r*u*h-muh-yohr
The pain occurs . . .	**Ağrısı tutuyor . . .**
	ah-r*u*h-s*u*h too-t*oo*-yohr
every quarter of an hour	**her çeyrek**
	hehr chehy-r*e*hk
every half-hour	**her yarım saat**
	hehr yah-r*u*hm sah-*a*ht

every hour	**her saat**
	hehr sah-*ah*t
every day	**her gün**
	hehr goohn
most of the time	**çoğu zaman**
	choh-*oo* zah-m*ah*n
I've had it for . . .	**. . . beri var**
	beh-r*ee* vahr
one hour/one day	**Bir saatten/Bir günden**
	beer sah-aht-tehn/beer goohn-d*eh*n
two hours/two days	**İki saatten/İki günden**
	ee-k*ee* sah-aht-tehn/ee-k*ee* goohn-dehn
It's a sharp pain	**Şiddetli bir ağrı**
	shee-deht-l*ee* beer ah-r*uh*
It's a dull pain	**Hafif bir ağrı**
	hah-f*ee*f beer ah-r*uh*
It's a nagging pain	**İçin için sızlıyor**
	ee-ch*ee*n ee-ch*ee*n suhz-l*uh*-yohr
I feel weak	**Kendimi güçsüz hissediyorum**
	kehn-dee-m*ee* goohch-s*ooh*z hees-seh-d*ee*-yoh-room
I feel feverish	**Ateşim var**
	ah-teh-sh*ee*m vahr
I feel dizzy	**Başım dönüyor**
	bah-sh*uh*m der-n*ooh*-yohr
I feel sick	**Midem bulanıyor**
	mee-d*eh*m boo-lah-n*uh*-yohr

Already under treatment for something else?

I take . . . regularly	**Muntazaman . . . alıyorum**
	moon-tah-zah-m*ah*n . . . ah-l*uh*-yoh-room
this medicine	**bu ilâcı**
	boo ee-lah-j*uh*
these pills	**bu hapı**
	boo hah-p*uh*
I have a heart condition	**Kalb hastasıyım**
	kahlb hahs-tah-suh-y*uh*m
I have haemorrhoids	**Hemoroidim var**
	heh-moh-roh-ee-d*ee*m vahr

I have rheumatism	**Romatizmam var** roh-mah-teez-m*a*hm vahr
I have diabetes	**Şeker hastasıyım** sheh-k*e*hr hahs-tah-suh-y*u*hm
I have asthma	**Astımım var** ahs-tuh-m*u*hm vahr
I am pregnant	**Hâmileyim** hah-mee-leh-y*ee*m
I'm allergic to (pencillin)	**(Penisiline) alerjim var** (peh-nee-see-lee-n*e*h) ah-lehr-j*ee*m vahr

Other essential expressions

Please can you help?	**Lütfen, yardım edebilir misiniz?** l*oo*ht-fehn yahr-d*u*hm eh-deh-bee- leer mee-see-n*ee*z
A doctor please	**Doktor, lütfen** dohk-t*o*hr l*oo*ht-fehn
A dentist	**Dişçi** deesh-ch*ee*
I don't speak Turkish	**Türkçe bilmiyorum** T*oo*hrk-cheh b*ee*l-mee-yoh-room
What time does . . . arrive?	**Saat kaçta ∴. . geliyor?** sah-aht kahch-t*a*h . . . gheh-lee- yohr
the doctor	**doktor** dohk-toh
the dentist	**dişçi** deesh-chee

From the doctor: key sentences to understand

Take this . . .	**. . . bundan alınız** boon-d*a*hn ah-luh-n*u*z
every day/every hour	**Her gün/Her saat** hehr goohn/hehr sah-*a*ht
(twice/four) times a day	**Günde (iki/dört) defa** goohn-d*e*h (ee-k*ee*/derrt) deh-f*a*h
Stay in bed	**Yatakta yatınız** yah-tahk-t*a*h yah-tuh-n*u*hz

Don't travel . . .	**. . . yolculuk etmeyiniz**
	yohl-joo-*look eht*-meh-yee-neez
for two (days/weeks)	**İki (gün/hafta) için**
	ee-k*ee* (goohn/hahf-t*ah*) ee-ch*een*
You must go to hospital	**Hastaneye gitmelisiniz**
	hahs-tah-neh-y*eh* gheet-meh-lee- see-n*eez*

Problems: complaints, loss, theft

ESSENTIAL INFORMATION

- Problems with:
  camping facilities, see p. 32
  household appliances, see p. 48
  health, see p. 86
  the car, see p. 99
- If the worse comes to the worst, find the police station. To ask the way, see p. 17.
- Look for:
  POLİS (Police)
  TURİZM POLİSİ (Tourist Police)
  POLİS KARAKOLU (police station)
- If you lose your passport, go to the nearest British Consulate.
- In an emergency dial 055 for the police and 000 for the fire brigade.

COMPLAINTS

I bought this . . .	**. . . bunu aldım**
	boo-n*oo* ahl-d*uhm*
today	**Bugün**
	boo-g*oohn*
yesterday	**Dün**
	doohn
on Monday	**Pazartesi günü**
	pah-zahr-teh-s*ee* gooh-n*ooh*

[*For days of the week, see p. 122*]

It's no good	**İyi değil**
	ee-yee deh-eel
Look	**Bakınız**
	bah-kuh-nuhz
Here [point]	**Burada**
	boo-rah-dah
Can you change it?	**Bunu değistirebilir misiniz?**
	boo-noo deh-ees-tee-reh-bee-leer mee-see-neez
Here is the receipt	**İşte makbuzu**
	eesh-teh mahk-boo-zoo
Can I have a refund?	**Paramı iade eder misiniz?**
	Pah-rah-muh ee-ah-deh eh-dehr mee-see-neez

LOSS

[*See also 'Theft' below: the lists are interchangeable*]

I have lost . . .	**. . . kaybettim**
	kay-beht-teem
my bag	**Çantamı**
	chahn-tah-muh
my bracelet	**Bileziğimi**
	bee-leh-zee-ee-mee
my camera	**Fotoğraf makinamı**
	foh-toh-rahf mah-kee-nah-muh
my car keys	**Araba anahtarlarımı**
	ah-rah-bah ah-nah-tahr-lah-ruh-muh
my driving licence	**Şoför ehliyetimi**
	shoh-fer eh-lee-yeh-tee-mee
my insurance certificate	**Sigorta poliçemi**
	see-gohr-tah poh-lee-cheh-mee
my jewellery	**Mücevherlerimi**
	mooh-jehv-hehr-leh-ree-mee
everything!	**Herşeyi**
	hehr-sheh-yee

THEFT

[*See also 'Loss' above: the lists are interchangeable*]

Someone has stolen . . .	. . . çaldılar
	chahl-duh-*la*hr
my car	**Arabamı**
	ah-rah-bah-m*uh*
my car radio	**Araba radyomu**
	ah-rah-b*ah* rahd-yoh-m*oo*
my keys	**Anahtarlarımı**
	ah-nah-tahr-lah-ruh-m*uh*
my money	**Paramı**
	pah-rah-m*uh*
my necklace	**Gerdanlığımı**
	ghehr-dahn-luh-uh-m*uh*
my passport	**Pasaportumu**
	pah-sah-pohr-too-m*oo*
my radio	**Radyomu**
	rahd-yoh-m*oo*
my tickets	**Biletlerimi**
	bee-leht-leh-ree-m*ee*
my travellers' cheques	**Seyahat çeklerimi**
	seh-yah-h*ah*t chehk-leh-ree-mee
my wallet	**Cüzdanımı**
	joohz-dah-nuh-m*uh*
my watch	**Saatimi**
	sah-aht-tee-m*ee*
my luggage	**Valizlerimi**
	vah-leez-leh-ree-m*ee*

LIKELY REACTIONS: key words to understand

Wait	**Bekleyiniz**
	behk-leh-yee-n*ee*z
When?	**Ne zaman?**
	neh zah-m*ah*n
Where?	**Nerede?**
	neh-reh-d*eh*
Name?	**Adı?**
	ah-d*uh*
Address?	**Adresi?**
	ah-dreh-s*ee*
I can't help you	**Ben yardım edemiyeceğim**
	behn yahr-d*uh*m eh-deh-mee-yeh-jeh-*ee*m

There's nothing I can do   **Benim yapabileceğim bir şey yok**
beh-neem yah-pah-bee-leh-jeh-eem
beer shehy yohk

The post office

ESSENTIAL INFORMATION

- To find a post office, see p. 17.
- The sign for post offices in Turkey is PTT
(black letters on a yellow background).

PTT

- The word for post office is **POSTANE**.
- Main post offices are usually open from 8.00 a.m. until 8.00 p.m.
In larger towns there is usually a post office open until midnight
and in the main cities one that stays open twenty-four hours a
day.
- Stamps are bought at the counter marked **PUL**.
- Post offices also deal with telephoning and telegrams.
- For poste restante you should show your passport at the counter
marked **POST RESTANT**.

WHAT TO SAY

To England, please   **İngiltere'ye lütfen**
een-gheel-teh-reh-yeh looht-fehn
[*Hand letters, cards or parcels over the counter*]
To Australia   **Avustralya'ya**
ah-voos-trahl-yah-yah
To the United States   **Amerika'ya**
ah-meh-ree-kah-yah
[*For other countries, see p. 127*]
How much is . . .   **. . . ne kadar?**
neh kah-dahr
     this parcel (to Canada)?   **Bu koli (Kanada'ya)**
boo koh-lee (kah-nah-dah-yah)

a letter (to Australia)?	**Bir mektub (Avustralya'ya)** beer mehk-toob (ah-voos-trahl-yah-yah)
a postcard to England	**Bir kartpostal (İngiltere'ye)** beer kahrt-pohs-tahl (een-gheel-teh-reh-yeh)
Air mail	**Uçak** oo-chahk
Surface mail	**Normal posta** nohr-mahl pohs-tah
One stamp, please	**Bir pul, lütfen** beer pool looht-fehn
Two stamps	**İki pul** ee-kee pool
One (one hundred) lira stamp	**Bir (yüz) liralık pul** beer (yoohz) lee-rah-luhk pool
I'd like to send a telegram	**Bir telgraf göndermek istiyorum** beer tehl-grahf ghern-dehr-mehk ees-tee-yoh-room

Telephoning

ESSENTIAL INFORMATION

- In order to make a telephone call from a public callbox you will need a jeton. These are obtainable from post offices (at the counter marked **JETON**) and also from street vendors (cigarette vendors usually sell jetons). Jetons come in three sizes: small, medium and large. Small jetons are used for local calls. Medium and large jetons are useful for long-distance and international calls. Callboxes usually have on them instructions in both Turkish and English. Phone cards are also available. These are called **TELEFON KARTI**.
- There are telephones at post offices; telephone boxes on the streets are yellow or orange.

- If you want to make a long-distance or international call without using jetons, you can do so at the post office. Write the number you want on a piece of paper and hand it over at the counter marked **TELEFON**. You will then be directed to a booth to take the call after it has been dialled for you. Payment for the call is made afterwards at the same counter.
- Most chemists – look for the sign **ECZANE** – have telephones for local calls. You will be given change or sold jetons to put in the slot, or asked to pay after you have made your call. Many local grocery shops have phones as well and operate the same system.
- To make local calls, just dial the number. To make calls outside the city limits or long distance, prefix the number with 9. To make international calls, dial 9, wait for the tone to change, then dial 9 again, followed by the international code and number.
- To call the UK, dial 9-9 44, then the number (minus any initial zero on the area code).
- To call the USA, dial 9-9 1, then the number.
- The telephone system in Turkey has a reputation for being somewhat erratic. It is now much improved; however, you may have to wait for a free line, or dial more than once before you are successful. Above all, be persistent and you will eventually get through!

WHAT TO SAY

Where can I make a telephone call?	**Nereden telefon edebiliyorum?** neh-reh-d*e*hn teh-leh-f*o*hn eh-deh-bee-l*ee*-yoh-room
Local/abroad	**Şehir içi/uluslararası** sheh-h*ee*r ee-ch*ee*/oo-loos-lahr-ah-rah-s*u*h
I'd like to call this number . . . [*show number*]	**Bu numarayı . . . istiyorum** boo noo-mah-rah-y*u*h . . . ees-t*ee*-yoh-room
in England	**İngiltere'de** een-gheel-t*e*h-reh-deh
in Canada	**Kanada'da** kah-n*a*h-dah-dah
in the USA	**Amerika'da** ah-meh-ree-k*a*h-dah

[*For other countries, see p. 127*]

Can you dial it for me, please?	**Benim için telefon edebilir misiniz?** beh-neem ee-cheen teh-leh-fohn eh-deh-bee-leer mee-see-neez
How much is it?	**Ne kadar?** neh kah-dahr
Hello!	**Alo!** ah-loh
May I speak to . . .	**. . . ile konuşmağa olur mu?** . . . ee-leh koh-noosh-mah-ah oh-loor moo
Extension . . .	**Dahili . . .** dah-hee-lee . . .
I'm sorry, I don't speak Turkish	**Özür dilerim, Türkçe bilmiyorum** er-zuohr dee-leh-reem toohrk-cheh beel-mee-yoh-room
Do you speak English?	**İngilizce biliyor musunuz?** Een-ghee-leez-jeh bee-lee-yohr moo-soo-nooz
Thank you, I'll phone back	**Teşekkür ederim, tekrar ararım** teh-shehk-koohr eh-deh-reem tehk-rahr ah-rah-ruhm
Goodbye	**Allahaısmarladık/Hoşça kal** ahl-lahs-mahr-lah-duhk/hohsh-chah kahl

LIKELY REACTIONS

That's (1,500) lira	**(Bir bin beş yüz) lira** (beer been behsh yoohz) lee-rah
Cabin number (3)	**Kulübe numarası (üç)** koo-looh-beh noo-mah-rah-suh (oohch)

[*For numbers, see p. 118*]

Don't hang up	**Ayrılmayınız** ay-ruhl-mah-yuh-nuhz
I'm trying to connect you	**Sizi bağlamağa uğraşıyorum** see-zee bah-lah-mah-ah oo-rah-shuh-yoh-room
You're through	**Konuşunuz** koh-noo-shoo-nooz

There's a delay	**Gecikme var** gheh-jeek-meh vahr
I'll try again	**Yine deneyeceğim** yee-neh deh-neh-yeh-jeh-eem

Travelers' checks and money

ESSENTIAL INFORMATION

- For finding the way to the bank or exchange bureau, see p. 17.
- Look for these words on buildings:
  BANKA ⎤ (bank)
  ... BANKASI ⎦
  KAMBİYO (change)
- Not all banks will cash Eurocheques. Those that do ask you to make it out in US$ (not Turkish lira or pounds sterling) and then give you TL at the current US$–TL rate.
- You will need your passport when changing money.
- Banks are open 9.00 a.m. – 12.00 noon, 1.30 p.m. – 4.00 p.m.

WHAT TO SAY

I'd like to cash . . .	**. . . bozdurmak istiyorum** bohz-door-mahk ees-tee-yoh-room
this travellers' cheque	**Bu seyahat çeki** boo seh-yah-haht cheh-kee
these travellers' cheques	**Bu seyahat çekleri** boo seh-yah-haht chehk-leh-ree
I'd like to change this into Turkish lira	**Bu Türk lirasına için bozdurmak istiyorum** boo toohrk lee-rah-suh-nah ee-cheen bohz-door-mahk ees-tee-yoh-room
Here's . . .	**İşte . . .** eesh-teh
my banker's card	**banka kartım** bahn-kah kahr-tuhm

my passport	**pasaportum**
	pah-sah-pohr-t*oo*m
What's the rate of exchange?	**Kur ne?**
	koor neh

LIKELY REACTIONS

Passport, please	**Pasaport, lütfen**
	pah-sah-p*o*hrt l*oo*ht-fehn
Sign here	**Burasını imzalayınız**
	boo-rah-suh-n*u*h eem-zah-lah-yuh-n*u*hz
Your banker's card, please	**Banka kartınızı, lütfen**
	b*a*hn-kah kahr-tuh-nuh-z*u*h l*o*oht-fehn
Go to the cash desk	**Vezneye gidiniz**
	vehz-neh-y*e*h ghee-dee-n*e*ez

Car travel

ESSENTIAL INFORMATION

- For finding a filling station or garage, see p. 17.
- Grades of petrol:
  Normal (83–87 octane)
  Süper (90–95 octane)
- For car repairs, look for:
  GARAJ (garage)
  OTOMOBİL TAMİRHANE (car repair workshop)
  OTOMOBİL TAMİRÇİ (car mechanic)
- Petrol stations may be able to help with minor repairs or direct you to a mechanic.
- The equivalent of the AA/RAC in Turkey is the: **Türkiye Turing ve Otomobil Kurumu** (Touring and Automobile Club of Turkey), Halâskârgazi Caddesi 364, Istanbul, Tel: 131 46 31.
- For unfamiliar road signs and warnings, see p. 114.

WHAT TO SAY

[For numbers, see p. 118]

(9) litres of . . .	**(Dokuz) litre . . .** (doh-k*oo*z) *lee*-treh
(2,000) lira of . . .	**(İki bin) lira . . .** (ee-k*ee* b*ee*n) *lee*-rah
standard/super/diesel	**normal/süper/dizel** nohr-m*ah*l/sooh-p*eh*r/dee-z*eh*l
Fill the tank, please	**Depoyu doldurunuz, lütfen** deh-poh-y*oo* dohl-doo-roo-n*oo*z *looh*t-fehn
Will you check . . .	**. . . kontrol eder misiniz?** kohn-tr*oh*l eh-d*eh*r mee-see-n*ee*z
the oil?	**Yağı** yah-*uh*
the battery?	**Aküyü** ah-kooh-y*oo*h
the radiator?	**Radyatörü** rahd-yah-ter-r*oo*h
the tyres?	**Lâstikleri** lahs-teek-leh-r*ee*
I've run out of petrol	**Benzinim bitmiş** behn-zee-n*ee*m beet-m*ee*sh
Can I borrow a can, please?	**Sizden teneke ödünç alabilir miyim?** seez-d*eh*n teh-neh-k*eh* er-d*oo*hnch ah-lah-bee-l*ee*r mee-y*ee*m
My car has broken down	**Arabam bozuldu** ah-rah-b*ah*m boh-zool-d*oo*
My car won't start	**Arabam çalışmıyor** ah-rah-b*ah*m chah-l*uh*sh-muh-y*oh*r
There's been an accident	**Kaza oldu** kah-z*ah* ohl-d*oo*
I've lost my car keys	**Araba anahtarlarımı kaybettim** ah-rah-b*ah* ah-nah-tahr-lah-ruh- m*uh* kay-beht-t*ee*m
My car is . . .	**Arabam . . .** ah-rah-b*ah*m
two kilometres away	**iki kilometre uzakta** ee-k*ee* kee-loh-meh-treh oo-zahk- t*ah*

three kilometres away	**üç kilometre uzakta** oohch kee-loh-meh-treh oo-zahk-tah
Can you help me, please?	**Bana yardım edebilir misiniz?** bah-nah yahr-duhm eh-deh-bee-leer mee-see-neez
Do you do repairs?	**Tamir yapıyor musunuz?** tah-meer yah-puh-yohr moo-soo-nooz
I have a puncture	**Lâstik patladı** lahs-teek paht-lah-duh
I have a broken windscreen	**Cam kırıldı** jahm kuh-ruhl-duh
I think the problem is here . . . [point]	**Problem şurada galiba** proh-blehm shoo-rah-dah gah-lee-bah
I don't know what's wrong	**Nesi var bilmiyorum** neh-see vahr beel-mee-yoh-room
Can you repair the fault?	**Tamir edebilir misiniz?** tah-meer eh-deh-bee-leer mee-see-neez
Can you come and look?	**Gelip bakabilir misiniz?** gheh-leep bah-kah-bee-leer mee-see-neez
Can you estimate the cost?	**Aşağı yukarı ne kadar tutar?** ah-shah-uh yoo-kah-ruh neh kah-dahr too-tahr
Can you write it down?	**Yazabilir misiniz?** yah-zah-bee-leer mee-see-neez
Do you accept these coupons	**Bu kuponları kabul ediyor musunuz?** boo koo-pohn-lah-ruh kah-bool eh-dee-yohr moo-soo-nooz
How long will the repair take?	**Tamir ne kadar sürer?** tah-meer neh kah-dahr sooh-rehr
When will the car be ready?	**Araba ne zaman hazır olacak?** ah-rah-bah neh zah-mahn hah-zuhr oh-lah-jahk
Can I see the bill?	**Hesaba bakabilir miyim?** heh-sah-bah bah-kah-bee-leer mee-yeem
This is my insurance document	**İşte poliçem** eesh-teh poh-lee-chehm

1 windscreen wipers	**silecekler** see-leh-jehk-*lehr*	11 fan belt	**vantilatör kayışı** vahn-tee-lah-ter kah-yuh-shuh
2 fuses	**sigortalar** see-gohr-tah-*lahr*	12 generator	**dinamo** dee-*nah*-moh
3 heater	**kalorifer** kah-loh-ree-*fehr*	13 brakes	**frenler** frehn-*lehr*
4 battery	**akü** ah-*kooh*	14 clutch	**debriyaj** deh-bree-*yahzh*
5 engine	**motor** moh-*tohr*	15 gear box	**şanjman** shahzh-*mahn*
6 fuel pump	**yağ pompası** yah pohm-pah-*suh*	16 steering	**direksiyon** dee-rehk-see-*yohn*
7 starter motor	**marş** mahrsh	17 ignition	**ateşleme** ah-tehsh-leh-*meh*
8 carburettor	**karbüratör** kahr-booh-rah-*ter*	18 transmission	**vites** vee-*tehs*
9 lights	**lambalar** lahm-bah-*lahr*	19 exhaust	**egzoz** ehg-*zohz*
10 radiator	**radyatör** rahd-yah-*ter*	20 indicator	**sinyal lambaları** seen-*yahl* lahm-bah-lah-*ruh*

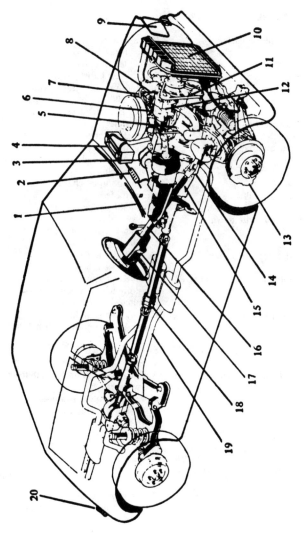

RENTING A CAR

Can I rent a car?	**Bir araba kiralıyabilir miyim?** beer ah-rah-bah kee-rah-luh-yah-bee-leer mee-yeem
I need a car . . .	**. . . bir araba istiyorum** beer ah-rah-bah ees-tee-yoh-room
for two people	**İki kişilik** ee-kee kee-shee-leek
for five people	**Beş kişilik** behsh kee-shee-leek
for one day	**Bir gün için** beer goohn ee-cheen
for five days	**Beş gün için** behsh goohn ee-cheen
for a week	**Bir hafta için** beer hahf-tah ee-cheen
Can you write down . . .	**. . . yazabiliyor musunuz?** yah-zah-bee-lee-yohr moo-soo-nooz
the deposit to pay?	**Depozito ne kadar** deh-poh-zee-toh neh kah-dahr
the charge per kilometre?	**Kilometre başına üçret ne kadar** kee-loh-meh-treh bah-shuh-nah oohch-reht neh kah-dahr
the daily charge?	**Günlük kirası ne kadar** goohn-loohk kee-rah-suh neh kah-dahr
the cost of insurance?	**Sigorta ne kadar** see-gohr-tah neh kah-dahr
Can I leave the car in Istanbul?	**Arabayı İstanbul'da birakabiliyor muyum?** ah-rah-bah-yuh ees-tahn-bool-dah bee-rah-kah-bee-lee-yohr moo-yoom
What documents do I need?	**Hangi belgelerim lâzım?** hahn-ghee behl-gheh-leh-reem lah-zhum

LIKELY REACTIONS

I don't do repairs	**Tamir yapmıyorum** tah-meer yahp-muh-yoh-room

Where's your car	**Arabanız nerede?**
	ah-rah-bah-n*u*hz neh-reh-d*e*h
What make is it?	**Hangi marka?**
	h*a*hn-ghee m*a*hr-kah
Come back (tomorrow/on Monday)	**(Yarın/Pazartesi günü) geliniz**
	(yah-r*u*hn/pah-zahr-teh-s*ee* goohn*oo*h) gheh-lee-n*ee*z

[*For days of the week, see p. 122*]

We don't hire cars	**Araba kiralamıyoruz**
	ah-rah-b*a*h kee-rah-l*a*h-muh-yoh-rooz
Your driving licence, please	**Şoför ehliyetiniz, lütfen**
	shoh-f*e*r eh-lee-yeh-tee-n*ee*z l*oo*ht-fehn
The mileage is unlimited	**Sınırsız kilometre**
	suh-nuhr-s*u*hz kee-loh-m*e*h-treh

Public transportation

ESSENTIAL INFORMATION

- For finding the way to the bus station, a bus stop, the railway station and a taxi rank, see p. 17.
- Istanbul can be reached by rail from all the major European cities. On the Asian side, one can travel by train, but this method of transport is slow and most people prefer to travel by long-distance buses, which are faster, cheaper and more frequent. The Turkish State Railways are called TCDD (**Türkiye Cumhuriyet Devlet Demiryolları**).
- There is a very extensive network of long-distance buses and mini-buses throughout the country. On inter-city buses you can book a seat in advance.
- Municipal buses are red. For these you need to buy tickets in advance to put in the box when you board the bus. Tickets are available at main terminals, and from vendors at all main bus stops. Tickets bought from vendors are very slightly more expensive.

- There are also privately run buses, which are blue. On these you can buy the ticket on board for cash or in exchange for municipal bus tickets.
- **Dolmuş**: a **dolmuş** is a shared car or taxi that travels a fixed route, for which you pay a fixed rate. The cars queue at **dolmuş** ranks, and as soon as a vehicle is full (**dolmuş** means 'full' in Turkish) it sets off. Destinations are marked on signs at the ranks or called out by the drivers. You can get off at any point along the route by asking the driver to stop. Some taxis operate in this way – but check by asking '**Dolmuşmu?**' before you get in.
- Taxis are usually very numerous in the cities and can be picked up at ranks or flagged down on the street. They all have meters, which by law must be in working order. It is wise to make sure that the driver has turned the meter on before setting out. At the end of the journey, pay what is on the meter plus a tip. (Drivers do not always expect tips, but it is becoming the practice to give them and they are much appreciated.)
- One of the great pleasures of Istanbul is travelling on the ferry-boats that link the European and Asian shores of the city and the villages along the shores of the Bosphorus. To get on board, you need to buy a jeton to pass through the turnstiles leading on to the landing stages. Jetons are sold at ticket windows by the turnstiles. If you want to avoid queuing you can also buy jetons from vendors (for a slightly higher price). Express ferries called **Deniz Otobüsleri** (sea buses) run on certain routes.
- Key words on signs (see also p. 114):
  BEKLEME SALONU (waiting room)
  BİLET GİŞESİ (ticket office)
  BÜFE (buffet)
  ÇIKIŞ (exit)
  DANIŞMA BÜROSU (information office)
  DENİZ OTOBÜSÜ (sea bus)
  DOLMUŞ
  EMANET (left luggage office)
  GİRİŞ (entrance)
  İSKELE (ferry landing)
  KAYIP EŞYALAR BÜROSU (lost property office)
  OTOBÜS DURAĞI (bus stop)
  PERON (platform)
  REZERVASYON BÜROSU (booking office)
  SIGARA İÇİLMEZ (no smoking)
  TAKSİ (taxi)

TARİFE (timetable)
TUVALETLER (toilets)
VAPUR (ferryboat)

WHAT TO SAY

Where does the bus (for Ankara) leave from?	**(Ankara'ya) otobüs nereden kalkıyor?** (ahn-kah-rah-yah) oh-toh-boohs neh-reh-dehn kahl-kuh-yohr
At what time does the bus leave (for Ankara)?	**Otobüs (Ankara'ya) saat kaçta kalkıyor?** oh-toh-boohs (ahn-kah-rah-yah) sah-aht kahch-tah kahl-kuh-yohr
At what time does the bus arrive (in Ankara)?	**(Ankara'ya) otobüs saat kaçta varıyor?** (ahn-kah-rah-yah) oh-toh-boohs sah-aht kahch-tah vah-ruh-yohr
Is this the bus (for Ankara)?	**(Ankara'ya) otobüs bu mu?** (ahn-kah-rah-yah) oh-toh-boohs boo moo
Where does the train (for Istanbul) leave from?	**(İstanbul'a) tren nereden kalkıyor?** (ees-tahn-boo-lah) trehn neh-reh-dehn kahl-kuh-yohr
At what time does the train leave (for Istanbul)?	**Tren (İstanbul'a) saat kaçta kalkıyor?** trehn (ees-tahn-boo-lah) sah-aht kahch-tah kahl-kuh-yohr
Is this the train (for Istanbul)?	**(İstanbul) treni bu mu?** (ees-tahn-bool) treh-nee boo moo
Do I have to change?	**Aktarma yapmam lâzım mı?** ahk-tahr-mah yahp-mahn lah-zuhm muh
Where does . . . leave from?	**. . . nereden kalkıyor?** neh-reh-dehn kahl-kuh-yohr
the bus	**Otobüs** oh-toh-boohs
the train	**Tren** trehn
the underground	**Tünel** tooh-nehl

the **dolmuş**	**Dolmuş** dohl-moosh
the ferryboat	**Vapur** vah-poor
for the airport	**hava meydanına** hah-vah mehy-dah-nuh-nah
for the mosque	**camiye** jah-mee-yeh
for the beach	**plaja** plah-zhah
for the market	**çarşıya** chahr-shuh-yah
for the railway station	**istasyona** ees-tahs-yoh-nah
for the town centre	**şehir merkezine** sheh-heer mehr-keh-zee-neh
for the town hall	**belediye dairesine** beh-leh-dee-yeh dah-ee-reh-see-neh
for the church	**kilise'ye** kee-lee-seh-yeh
for the swimming pool	**yüzme havuzuna** yoohz-meh hah-voo-zoo-nah
Is this . . .	**. . . bu mu?** boo moo
the bus for the market place?	**Çarşıya otobüs** chahr-shuh-yah oh-toh-boohs
the **dolmuş** for the station?	**İstasyona dolmuş** ees-tahs-yoh-nah dohl-moosh
Where can I get a taxi?	**Taksi nerede bulabilirim?** tahk-see neh-reh-deh boo-lah-bee-lee-reem
Can you put me off at the right stop, please?	**Beni doğru durakta indiriniz, lütfen?** beh-nee doh-roo doo-rahk-tah een-dee-ree-neez looht-fehn
Can I book a seat?	**Yer ayırtabiliyor muyum?** yehr ah-yuhr-tah-bee-lee-yohr moo-yoom
A single	**Yalnız gidiş** yahl-nuhz ghee-deesh

A return	**Gidiş dönüş** ghee-*deesh* der-n*oosh*
First class	**Birinci mevki** bee-reen-j*ee* mehv-k*ee*
Second class	**İkinci mevki** ee-keen-j*ee* mehv-k*ee*
One adult	**Bir kişi** beer kee-sh*ee*
Two adults	**İki kişi** ee-k*ee* kee-sh*ee*
and one child	**ve bir çocuk** veh beer choh-j*ook*
and two children	**ve iki çocuk** veh ee-k*ee* choh-j*ook*
How much is it?	**Ne kadar?** neh kah-d*ah*r

LIKELY REACTIONS

Over there	**Orada** oh-rah-d*ah*
Here	**Burada** boo-rah-d*ah*
Platform (1)	**Peron (bir)** peh-r*oh*n (beer)
(At 4) o'clock	**Saat (dörtte)** sah-aht (derrt-teh)
[*For times, see p. 120*] Change (at Ankara)	**(Ankara'da) aktarma yapınız** (*ah*n-kah-rah-dah) ahk-tahr-m*ah* yah-puh-n*uh*z
Change (at the market)	**Carşıda aktarma yapınız** chahr-shuh-d*ah* ahk-tahr-m*ah* yah- puh-n*uh*z
This is your stop	**Durağınız bu** doo-rah-uh-n*uh*z boo
There's only second class	**Yalnız ikinci mevki var** yahl-n*uh*z ee-keen-j*ee* mehv-k*ee* vahr
There's a supplement	**Fark ödemiz lâzım** fahrk er-deh-m*ee*z l*ah*-zuhm

Leisure

ESSENTIAL INFORMATION

- For finding the way to a place of entertainment, see p. 17.
- For times of day, see p. 120.
- For important signs, see p. 114.

WHAT TO SAY

At what time does . . . open?	**Saat kaçta . . . açılıyor** sah-*a*ht kahch-t*a*h . . . ah-chuh-l*u*h-yohr
the art gallery	**sanat galerisi** sah-n*a*ht gah-leh-ree-s*ee*
the cinema	**sinema** see-neh-m*a*h
the concert hall	**konser salonu** kohn-s*e*hr sah-loh-n*oo*
the disco	**diskotek** dees-koh-t*e*hk
the museum	**müze** mooh-z*e*h
the night club	**gece kulübü** gheh-j*e*h koo-looh-b*oo*h
the sports stadium	**stadyum** stahd-y*oo*m
the swimming pool	**yüzme havuzu** yoohz-m*e*h hah-voo-z*oo*
the theatre	**tiyatro** tee-y*a*h-troh
the zoo	**hayvanat bahçesi** hay-vah-n*a*ht bah-cheh-s*ee*
At what time does . . . close?	**Saat kaçta . . . kapanıyor?** sah-aht kahch-t*a*h . . . kah-pah-n*u*h-yohr
the art gallery	**sanat galerisi** sah-n*a*ht gah-leh-ree-s*ee*
[See above list]	
At what time does . . . start?	**Saat kaçta . . . başlıyor?** sah-*a*ht kahch-t*a*h . . . bahsh-l*u*h-yohr

the cabaret	**kabare**
	kah-bah-reh
the concert	**konser**
	kohn-sehr
the film	**filim**
	fee-leem
the match	**maç**
	mahch
the play	**piyes**
	pee-yehs
the wrestling	**güreş**
	gooh-rehsh
How much is it . . .	**. . . ne kadar?**
	neh kah-dahr
for an adult?	**Bir kişi**
	beer kee-shee
for a child?	**Bir çocuk**
	beer choh-jook
Two adults, please	**İki kişi, lütfen**
	ee-kee kee-shee looht-fehn
Three children, please	**Üç çocuk, lütfen**
	oohch choh-jook looht-fehn
Stalls/circle	**Koltuk/balkon**
	kohl-took/bahl-kohn
Do you have . . .	**. . . var mı?**
	vahr muh
a programme?	**Program**
	proh-grahm
a guide book?	**Rehber**
	reh-behr
Where's the toilet, please?	**Tuvalet nerede, lütfen**
	too-wah-leht neh-reh-deh looht-fehn
Where's the cloakroom?	**Gardırop nerede?**
	gahr-duh-rohp neh-reh-deh
I would like lessons in . . .	**. . . dersleri almak istiyorum**
	dehrs-leh-ree ahl-mahk ees-tee-yoh-room
skiing	**Ski/Kayak**
	skee/kah-yahk
sailing	**Yelken**
	yehl-kehn

water skiing	**Su kayağı** soo kah-yah-*u*h
sub-aqua diving	**Sualtı sporu** soo-ahl-t*u*h spoh-r*oo*
Can I rent...	**. . . kiralıyabilir miyim?** kee-rah-luh-yah-bee-l*e*er mee-y*e*em
some skis?	**Kayak** kah-y*a*hk
some ski-boots?	**Kayak çizmesi** kah-y*a*hk cheez-meh-s*ee*
a boat?	**Bir sandal** beer sahn-dahl
a fishing rod?	**Bir olta kamışı** beer ohl-t*a*h kah-muh-sh*u*h
a deck chair?	**Bir şezlong** beer shehz-l*o*hng
a sun umbrella?	**Bir güneş şemsiyesi** beer gooh-n*e*hsh shehm-see-yeh-s*ee*
the necessary equipment?	**Gerekli malzeme** gheh-rehk-l*ee* mahl-zeh-m*e*h
How much is it . . .	**. . . ne kadar?** neh kah-d*a*hr
per day/per hour?	**Günü/Saati** gooh-n*oo*h/sah-*a*h-tee
Do I need a licence?	**Ruhsat lâzım mı?** roo-hs*a*ht lah-zuhm muh

Asking if things are allowed

ESSENTIAL INFORMATION

Excuse me, please	**Affedersiniz, efendim** ahf-feh-dehr-see-n*ee*z eh-f*e*hn-deem
Can one . . .	**. . . mi?** mee

camp here?	**Burada kamp kurulabilir**
	boo-rah-d*a*h kahmp koo-roo-lah-bee-l*ee*r
come in?	**Buraya girilebilir**
	boo-rah-y*a*h ghee-ree-leh-bee-l*ee*r
dance here?	**Burada dans edilebilir**
	boo-rah-d*a*h dahns eh-dee-leh-bee-l*ee*r
fish here?	**Burada balık tutulabilir**
	boo-rah-d*a*h bah-l*u*hk too-too-lah-bee-l*ee*r
get a drink here?	**Burada içki içilebilir**
	boo-rah-d*a*h eech-k*ee* ee-chee-leh-bee-l*ee*r
get out this way?	**Buradan çıkılabilir**
	boo-rah-d*a*hn chuh-kuh-lah-bee-l*ee*r
get something to eat here?	**Burada bir şey yenilebilir**
	boo-rah-d*a*h beer shehy yeh-nee-leh-bee-l*ee*r
leave one's things here?	**Burada eşya bırakılabilir**
	boo-rah-d*a*h ehsh-y*a*h bee-rah-kuh-lah-bee-l*ee*r
look around here?	**Etrafa bakılabilir**
	eh-trah-f*a*h bah-kuh-lah-bee-l*ee*r
park here?	**Burada park edilebilir**
	boo-rah-d*a*h pahrk eh-dee-leh-bee-l*ee*r
sit here?	**Burada oturulabilir**
	boo-rah-d*a*h oh-too-roo-lah-bee-l*ee*r
smoke here?	**Burada sigara içilebilir**
	boo-rah-d*a*h see-g*a*h-rah ee-chee-leh-bee-l*ee*r
swim here?	**Burada yüzülebilir**
	boo-rah-d*a*h yooh-zooh-leh-bee-l*ee*r
take photos here?	**Burada fotoğraf çekilebilir**
	boo-rah-d*a*h foh-toh-r*a*hf cheh-kee-leh-bee-l*ee*r
telephone here?	**Buradan telefon edilebilir**
	boo-rah-d*a*hn teh-leh-f*o*hn eh-dee-leh-bee-l*ee*r

wait here?

Burada beklenilebilir
boo-rah-d*a*h behk-leh-nee-leh-bee-
   lee*r*

LIKELY REACTIONS

Yes, certainly

Tabii, olur
tah-bee-*ee* oh-l*oo*r

No, certainly not

Olmaz
ohl-m*a*hz

I think so

Sanıyorum
sah-n*u*h-yoh-room

Of course

Tabii
tah-bee-*ee*

Yes, but be careful

Evet, ama dikkat!
*e*h-veht ah-m*a*h deek-k*a*ht

I don't think so

Sanmıyorum
s*a*hn-muh-yoh-room

Not normally

Çoğunlukla, hayır
choh-oon-look-l*a*h h*a*h-yuhr

Sorry

Özür dilerim
er-z*oo*hr dee-leh-r*ee*m

Reference

SIGN LANGUAGE

• Key words on signs for drivers, pedestrians, travellers, shoppers and overnight guests.

AÇIK	Open
ASANSÖR	Lift
AZAMİ SÜRAT	Speed limit
BAYANLAR	Ladies
BAYLAR	Gentlemen
BENZİN İSTASYONU	Petrol station

BİLETLER	Tickets
BOŞ	Vacant
BOŞ YER YOK	No vacancies
ÇALINIZ	Ring
ÇEKİNİZ	Pull
ÇIKILIR	Way out
ÇIKIŞ	Exit
DANIŞMA	Information
DENİZE GİRİLMEZ	No bathing
DİKKAT	Attention
DİKKAT KÖPEK VAR	Beware of the dog
DOKUNMAYINIZ	Do not touch
DOLU/DOLMUŞTUR	Full
DUR	Stop!
DURAK	Stop (as in bus stop)
DURMAK YASAKTIR	No stopping
EMÂNET	Left luggage
GEÇ	Cross (now)
GEÇİT	Crossing
GEÇMEK YASAKTIR	No overtaking
GERİ DÖNÜLMEZ	No U-turn
GİRİLİR	Way in
GİRİLMEZ	No entry
GİRİNİZ	Enter
GİRİŞ	Entrance
GİRİŞ SERBESTTİR	Entrance free
GİRMEK YASAK(TIR)	Entry forbidden
GİŞE	Ticket office
GÜMRÜK	Customs
HAREKET	Departure
İÇİLMEZ	Not for drinking
İÇME SUYU	Drinking water
İLK YARDIM	First aid
İMDAT ÇIKIŞI	Emergency exit
İSKELE	Landing stage (ferry)
İTİNİZ	Push
İZİNSİZ GİRİLMEZ	No unauthorized entry
JETON GİŞELERİ	Jeton counter
KAMP YAPMAK YASAK	No camping
KAPALI	Closed
KARAKOL	Police station
KAVŞAK	Road junction

KILAVUZ	Guide
KİRALIK	For rent
KUŞET	Couchette
LOKANTA VAGONU	Dining car
MEŞGUL	Occupied
ÖLÜM TEHLİKESİ	Danger of death
OTOBÜS DURAĞI	Bus stop
ÖZEL	Private
PARK YAPILMAZ	No parking
PERONLAR	Platforms
POLİS	Police
SAĞDAN GİDİNİZ	Keep right
SATILIK	For sale
SATIŞLAR	Sales
SICAK	Hot
SİGARA İÇİLMEZ	No smoking
SOĞUK	Cold
SOLDAN GİDİNİZ	Keep left
SON	End
TAŞIT GİREMEZ	No entry for vehicles
TEHLİKE	Danger
TEHLİKELİ MADDE	Dangerous substance
TEK İSTİKAMET	One way
TEK YÖN	One way
TERCÜMAN	Interpreter/translator
TRAFİK POLİSİ	Traffic police
TREN YOLU GEÇİDİ	Level crossing
TUTULMUŞ	Reserved
TUVALET	Toilet
VARIŞ	Arrival
VEZNE	Cashier
VİRAJ	Bend
YASAK(TIR)	Prohibited
YATAKLI VAGON	Sleeping car
YAVAŞ	Slow
YAYA GEÇİDİ	Pedestrian crossing
YOLDA ÇALIŞMA	Road works
YOL KAPALIDIR	Road closed
YOL TAMİRATI	Road repairs

ABBREVIATIONS

AA	**Anadolu Ajansı**	Anatolia Agency (a press agency)
ABD	**Amerika Birleşik Devletleri**	USA
Ank.	**Ankara**	Ankara
apt.	**apartman**	apartment house
As.	**Askeri**	Military
As.İz.	**Askeri İnzibat**	Military Police
ass.	**asistan**	assistant
AŞ	**Anonim Şirketi**	Ltd
B.	**Bay**	Mr
B.	**Batı**	West
BM	**Birleşmiş Milletler**	United Nations
BMM	**Büyük Millet Meclisi**	Grand National Assembly (Turkish parliament)
Bn	**Bayan**	Mrs, Miss, Ms
Bul.	**Bulvar**	Boulevard
Cad.	**Cadde**	Avenue
D.	**Doğu**	East
DDY	**Devlet Deniz Yolları**	Turkish State Maritime Lines
Doc.	**Doçent**	Assistant Professor
Dr	**Doktor**	Doctor
G.	**Güney**	South
Gen.	**General**	General
gr.	**gram**	gram
İETT	**İstanbul Elektrik Tramvay Tünel**	Istanbul Municipal Transport
İst.	**İstanbul**	Istanbul
K.	**Kuzey**	North
KDV	**Katma Değer Vergisi**	VAT
kg.	**kilogram**	kilogram
km.	**kilometre**	kilometre
Koll.Şti.	**Kollektif Şirketi**	Ltd
L.	**lira**	lira
m.	**metre**	metre
Mah.	**Mahalle**	district, borough, ward
Mah.	**Mahkeme**	law court
MÖ	**Milâttan önce**	BC
MS	**Milâttan sonra**	AD
No.	**numara**	number

Ord.Prof.	**Ordinaryüs Profesör**	Professor
Ort.	**Ortaklık**	Private Company
PK	**Posta Kutusu**	post box
PTT	**Posta Telgraf Telefon**	Post, Telegraph and Telephone Office
s.	**sayfa**	page
sm.	**santimetre**	centimetre
Sok.	**Sokak**	Street
TBMM	**Türkiye Büyük Millet Meclisi**	Turkish Grand National Assembly (parliament)
TC	**Türkiye Cumhuriyeti**	Republic of Turkey
TCDD	**Türkiye Cumhuriyeti Devlet Demiryolları**	Turkish State Railways
TDK	**Türk Dil Kurumu**	Turkish Language Society
Tel.	**telefon**	telephone
Telf.	**telefon**	telephone
Telg.	**telgraf**	telegraph
THY	**Türk Hava Yolları**	Turkish Airlines
TM	**Türk Malı**	Made in Turkey
TL	**Türk lirası**	Turkish lira
TRT	**Türkiye Radyo Televizyon Kurumu**	Turkish Radio and Television Corporation
TTOK	**Türkiye Turing ve Otomobil Kurumu**	Touring and Automobile Club of Turkey
v.d.	**ve devamı**	and so on
v.s.	**ve saire**	etc.

NUMBERS

Cardinal numbers

0	**sıfır**	suh-f*uh*r
1	**bir**	beer
2	**iki**	ee-k*ee*
3	**üç**	oohch
4	**dört**	derrt
5	**beş**	behsh
6	**altı**	alh-t*uh*
7	**yedi**	yeh-d*ee*
8	**sekiz**	seh-k*ee*z

9	**dokuz**	doh-kooz
10	**on**	ohn
11	**on bir**	ohn beer
12	**on iki**	ohn ee-kee
13	**on üç**	ohn oohch
14	**on dört**	ohn derrt
15	**on beş**	ohn behsh
16	**on altı**	ohn ahl-tuh
17	**on yedi**	ohn yeh-dee
18	**on sekiz**	ohn seh-keez
19	**on dokuz**	ohn doh-kooz
20	**yirmi**	yeer-mee
21	**yirmi bir**	yeer-mee beer
22	**yirmi iki**	yeer-mee ee-kee
23	**yirmi üç**	yeer-mee oohch
24	**yirmi dört**	yeer-mee derrt
25	**yirmi beş**	yeer-mee behsh
30	**otuz**	oh-tooz
35	**otuz beş**	oh-tooz behsh
40	**kırk**	kuhrk
45	**kırk beş**	kuhrk behsh
50	**elli**	ehl-lee
55	**elli beş**	ehl-lee behsh
60	**altmış**	ahlt-muhsh
65	**altmış beş**	ahlt-muhsh behsh
70	**yetmiş**	yeht-meesh
75	**yetmiş beş**	yeht-meesh behsh
80	**seksen**	sehk-sehn
85	**seksen beş**	sehk-sehn behsh
90	**doksan**	dohk-sahn
95	**doksan beş**	dohk-sahn behsh
100	**yüz**	yoohz
105	**yüz beş**	yoohz behsh
115	**yüz on beş**	yoohz ohn behsh
125	**yüz yirmi beş**	yoohz yeer-mee behsh
200	**iki yüz**	ee-kee yoohz
205	**iki yüz beş**	ee-kee yoohz behsh
215	**iki yüz on beş**	ee-kee yoohz ohn behsh
300	**üç yüz**	oohch yoohz
400	**dört yüz**	derrt yoohz
500	**beş yüz**	behsh yoohz
600	**altı yüz**	ahl-tuh yoohz

700	**yedi yüz**	yeh-d*ee* yoohz
800	**sekiz yüz**	seh-k*ee*z yoohz
900	**dokuz yüz**	doh-k*ooz* yoohz
1000	**bin**	been
2000	**iki bin**	ee-k*ee* been
5000	**beş bin**	behsh been
10,000	**on bin**	ohn been
100,000	**yüz bin**	yoohz been
1,000,000	**bir milyon**	beer meel-y*o*hn

Ordinal numbers

1st	**birinci**	bee-reen-j*ee*
2nd	**ikinci**	ee-keen-j*ee*
3rd	**üçüncü**	ooh-choohn-j*oo*h
4th	**dördüncü**	derr-doohn-j*oo*h
5th	**beşinci**	beh-sheen-j*ee*
6th	**altıncı**	ahl-tuhn-j*u*h
7th	**yedinci**	yeh-deen-j*ee*
8th	**sekizinci**	seh-kee-zeen-j*ee*
9th	**dokuzuncu**	doh-koo-zoon-j*oo*
10th	**onuncu**	oh-noon-j*oo*
11th	**on birinci**	ohn bee-reen-j*ee*
12th	**on ikinci**	ohn ee-keen-j*ee*

TIME

What time is it?	**Saat kaç**
	sah-*a*ht kahch
It's . . .	(This is not translated in Turkish)
one o'clock	**Saat bir**
	sah-*a*ht beer
two o'clock	**Saat iki**
	sah-*a*ht ee-k*ee*
three o'clock	**Saat üç**
	sah-*a*ht oohch
four o'clock in the morning	**Sabah saat dört**
	sah-b*a*h sah-*a*ht derrt
in the afternoon	**Öğleden sonra . . .**
	er-leh-d*e*hn s*o*hn-rah
in the evening	**Akşam . . .**
	ahk-sh*a*hm

at night	**Gece . . .**
	gheh-j*eh*
It's . . .	(This is not translated in Turkish)
noon	**Öğle**
	er-leh
half past twelve	**Yarım**
	yah-r*uh*m
midnight	**Gece yarısı**
	gheh-j*eh* yah-ruh-s*uh*
It's . . .	(This is not translated in Turkish)
five past five	**Beşi beş geçiyor**
	beh-sh*ee* behsh gheh-ch*ee*-yohr
ten past five	**Beşi on geçiyor**
	beh-sh*ee* ohn gheh-ch*ee*-yohr
a quarter past five	**Beşi çeyrek geçiyor**
	beh-shee chehy-r*eh*k gheh-ch*ee*-yohr
twenty past five	**Beşi yirmi geçiyor**
	Beh-sh*ee* yeer-m*ee* gheh-ch*ee*-yohr
twenty-five past five	**Beşi yirmi beş geçiyor**
	beh-sh*ee* yeer-m*ee* behsh gheh-ch*ee*-yohr
half past five	**Beş buçuk**
	behsh boo-ch*ook*
twenty-five to six	**Altıya yirmi beş var**
	ahl-tuh-y*ah* yeer-m*ee* behsh var
twenty to six	**Altıya yirmi var**
	ahl-tuh-y*ah* yeer-m*ee* vahr
a quarter to six	**Altıya çeyrek var**
	ahl-tuh-y*ah* chehy-r*eh*k vahr
ten to six	**Altıya on var**
	ahl-tuh-y*ah* ohn vahr
five to six	**Altıya beş var**
	ahl-tuh-y*ah* behsh var
At what time . . . (does the bus leave)?	**Saat kaçta . . . (otobüs kalkıyor)?**
	sah-*ah*t kahch-t*ah* . . . (oh-toh-b*oo*hs kahl-k*uh*-yohr)
At . . .	(In Turkish the 'at' is translated by the suffix **de/da** or **te/ta** added to the end of the number.)
13.00	**On üçte**
	ohn oohch-t*eh*

14.05	**On dört beşte** ohn derrt behsh-t*e*h
15.10	**On beş onda** ohn behsh ohn-d*a*h
16.15	**On yedi on beşte** ohn yeh-d*ee* ohn behsh-t*e*h
17.20	**On yedi yirmide** ohn yeh-d*ee* yeer-mee-deh
18.25	**On sekiz yirmi beşte** ohn seh-k*ee*z yeer-m*ee* behsh-t*e*h
19.30	**On dokuz otuzda** ohn doh-k*oo*z oh-tooz-d*a*h
20.35	**Yirmi otuz beşte** yeer-m*ee* oh-t*oo*z behsh-t*e*h
21.40	**Yirmi bir kırkta** yeer-m*ee* beer kuhrk-t*a*h
22.45	**Yirmi iki kırk beşte** yeer-m*ee* ee-k*ee* kuhrk behsh-t*e*h
23.50	**Yirmi üç ellide** yeer-m*ee* oohch ehl-lee-deh
00.55	**Sıfır elli beşte** suh-f*u*hr ehl-l*ee* behsh-t*e*h
in ten minutes	**on dakkika sonra** ohn dahk-k*ee*-kah s*o*hn-rah
in a quarter of an hour	**bir çeyrek saat sonra** beer chehy-r*e*hk sah-*a*ht s*o*hn-rah
in half an hour	**yarım saat sonra** yah-r*u*hm sah-*a*ht s*o*hn-rah
in three-quarters of an hour	**üç çeyrek saat sonra** oohch chehy-r*e*hk sah-*a*ht s*o*hn-rah

DAYS

Monday	**Pazartesi** pah-z*a*hr-teh-see
Tuesday	**Salı** sah-l*u*h
Wednesday	**Çarşamba** chahr-sh*a*hm-bah
Thursday	**Perşembe** pehr-sh*e*hm-beh
Friday	**Cuma** joo-m*a*h

Saturday	**Cumartesi**
	joo-mahr-teh-see
Sunday	**Pazar**
	pah-zahr
last Monday	**geçen pazartesi**
	gheh-chehn pah-zahr-teh-see
next Tuesday	**gelecek salı**
	gheh-leh-jehk sah-luh
on Wednesday	**Çarsamba günü**
	chahr-shahm-bah gooh-nooh
on Thursdays	**Perşembe günleri**
	pehr-shehm-beh goohn-leh-ree
until Friday	**Cumaya kadar**
	joo-mah-yah kah-dahr
until Saturday	**Cumartesiye kadar**
	joo-mahr-teh-see-yeh kah-dahr
before Sunday	**Pazardan önce**
	pah-zahr-dahn ern-jeh
before Monday	**Pazartesiden önce**
	pah-zahr-teh-see-dehn ern-jeh
after Wednesday	**Çarşambadan sonra**
	chahr-shahm-bah-dahn sohn-rah
after Thursday	**Perşembeden sonra**
	pehr-shehm-beh-dehn sohn-rah
the day before yesterday	**evvelki gün**
	ehv-vehl-kee goohn
two days ago	**iki gün önce**
	ee-kee goohn ern-jeh
yesterday	**dün**
	doohn
yesterday morning	**dün sabah**
	doohn sah-bah
yesterday afternoon	**dün öğleden sonra**
	doohn er-leh-dehn sohn-rah
last night	**dün gece**
	doohn gheh-jeh
today	**bugün**
	boo-goohn
this morning	**bu sabah**
	boo sah-bah
this afternoon	**bu öğleden sonra**
	boo er-leh-dehn sohn-rah

tonight	**bu gece**
	boo gheh-jeh
tomorrow	**yarın**
	yah-ruhn
tomorrow morning	**yarın sabah**
	yah-ruhn sah-bah
tomorrow afternoon	**yarın öğleden sonra**
	yah-ruhn er-leh-dehn sohn-rah
tomorrow evening	**yarın akşam**
	yah-ruhn ahk-shahm
tomorrow night	**yarın gece**
	yah-ruhn gheh-jeh
the day after tomorrow	**öbür gün**
	er-boohr goohn

MONTHS AND DATES

January	**Ocak**
	oh-jahk
February	**Şubat**
	shoo-baht
March	**Mart**
	mahrt
April	**Nisan**
	nee-sahn
May	**Mayıs**
	mah-yuhs
June	**Haziran**
	hah-zee-rahn
July	**Temmuz**
	tehm-muhz
August	**Ağustos**
	ah-oos-tohs
September	**Eylül**
	ehy-loohl
October	**Ekim**
	eh-keem
November	**Kasım**
	kah-suhm
December	**Aralık**
	ah-rah-luhk

in January	**ocakta**
	oh-jahk-t*a*h
in June	**haziranda**
	hah-zee-rahn-d*a*h
in September	**eylülde**
	ey-loohl-d*e*h
until February	**şubata kadar**
	shoo-baht-t*a*h kah-d*a*hr
until July	**temmuze kadar**
	tehm-moo-z*e*h kah-d*a*hr
before March	**marttan önce**
	mahrt-t*a*hn ern-j*e*h
before April	**nisandan önce**
	nee-sahn-d*a*hn ern-j*e*h
after May	**mayıstan sonra**
	mah-yuhs-t*a*hn s*o*hn-rah
during June	**haziran içinde**
	hah-zee-r*a*hn ee-cheen-d*e*h
not before July	**temmuzdan önce değil**
	teh-mooz-d*a*hn ern-j*e*h deh-*ee*l
the beginning of August	**ağustosun başı**
	ah-oos-toh-s*oo*n bah-sh*u*h
the middle of September	**eylülün ortası**
	ey-looh-l*oo*hn ohr-tah-s*u*h
the end of October	**ekimin sonu**
	eh-kee-m*ee*n soh-n*oo*
last month	**geçen ay**
	gheh-ch*e*hn ay
this month	**bu ay**
	boo ay
next month	**gelecek ay**
	gheh-leh-j*e*hk ay
in spring	**ilkbaharda**
	eelk-bah-hahr-d*a*h
in summer	**yazda**
	yahz-d*a*h
in autumn	**sonbaharda**
	sohn-bah-hahr-d*a*h
in winter	**kışta**
	kuhsh-t*a*h
this year	**bu yıl**
	boo yuhl

last year	**geçen yıl**
	gheh-chehn yuhl
next year	**gelecek yıl**
	gheh-leh-jehk yuhl
in 1985	**bin dokuz yüz seksen beşte**
	been doh-kooz yoohz sehk-sehn behsh-teh
in 1992	**bin dokuz yüz doksan ikide**
	been doh-kooz yoohz dohk-sahn ee-kee-deh
What's the date today?	**Bugün tarihi ne**
	boo-goohn tah-ree-hee neh
It's 6th March	**Altı mart**
	ahl-tuh mahrt
12th April	**On iki nisan**
	ohn ee-kee nee-sahn
21st August	**Yirmi bir ağustos**
	yeer-mee beer ah-oos-tohs

Public holidays

1 January	**Yılbaşı**	New Year's Day
23 April	**23 Nisan Çocuk Bayramı**	National Sovereignty and Children's Day
19 May	**Gençlik ve Spor Bayramı**	Youth and Sport Day
30 August	**Zafer Bayramı**	Victory Day
28–9 October	**Cumhuriyet Bayramı**	Republic Days

Religious festivals

- The two most important festivals in the Islamic calendar in Turkey are the **Şeker Bayramı** (Sugar Festival), when Muslims celebrate the end of **Ramadan** – the month of fasting – with three and a half days of holiday and feasting; and, three months later, the **Kurban Bayramı** (Feast of the Sacrifice), which lasts for four and a half days. Since the times of the festivals are calculated according to the lunar calendar they fall on different days every year, gradually moving through all the months of the year.
- The Christians and Jews of Turkey also, of course, celebrate their own holy days at the appropriate times.

COUNTRIES AND NATIONALITIES

Countries

Australia	**Avustralya** ah-voos-tr*a*hl-yah
Austria	**Avusturya** ah-v*oo*s-toor-yah
Belgium	**Belçika** behl-chee-k*a*h
Britain	**Britanya** bree-t*a*hn-yah
Canada	**Kanada** kah-n*a*h-dah
Czechoslovakia	**Çekoslovakya** cheh-koh-sloh-vahk-y*a*h
East Africa	**Doğu Afrika** doh-*oo* ahf-ree-k*a*h
East Germany	**Doğu Almanya** doh-*oo* ahl-m*a*hn-yah
Eire	**İrlanda** eer-l*a*hn-dah
England	**İngiltere** een-gheel-t*e*h-reh
France	**Fransa** fr*a*hn-sah
Greece	**Yunanistan** yoo-nah-nee-st*a*hn
India	**Hindistan** heen-dee-st*a*hn
Italy	**İtalya** ee-t*a*hl-yah
Luxembourg	**Luksemburg** loohk-sehm-b*oo*rg
Netherlands	**Holanda** hoh-l*a*hn-dah
New Zealand	**Yeni Zelanda** yeh-n*ee* zeh-l*a*hn-dah
Northern Ireland	**Kuzey İrlanda** koo-z*e*hy eer-l*a*hn-dah
Pakistan	**Pakistan** p*a*h-kee-stahn

Poland	**Polonya**
	poh-lohn-yah
Portugal	**Portekiz**
	pohr-teh-keez
Scotland	**İskoçya**
	ees-kohch-yah
South Africa	**Güney Afrika**
	gooh-nehy ahf-ree-kah
Spain	**İspanya**
	ees-pahn-yah
Switzerland	**İsviçre**
	ees-veech-reh
Turkey	**Türkiye**
	toohr-kee-yeh
USSR	**Sovyetler**
	sohv-yeht-lehr
Wales	**Galler**
	gahl-lehr
West Germany	**Batı Almanya**
	bah-tuh ahl-mahn-yah
West Indies	**Antiller**
	ahn-teel-lehr
Yugoslavia	**Yugoslavya**
	yoo-goh-slahv-yah

Nationalities

American	**Amerikalı**
	ah-meh-ree-kah-luh
Australian	**Avustralyalı**
	ah-voos-trahl-yah-luh
British	**Britanyalı**
	bree-tahn-yah-luh
Canadian	**Kanadalı**
	kah-nah-dah-luh
East African	**Doğu Afrikalı**
	doh-oo ahf-ree-kah-luh
English	**İngiliz**
	een-ghee-leez
Greek	**Yunanlı**
	yoo-nahn-luh

Indian	**Hintli**
	heent-*lee*
Irish	**İrlandalı**
	eer-l*a*hn-dah-luh
New Zealander	**Yeni Zelandalı**
	yeh-n*ee* zeh-l*a*hn-dah-luh
Pakistani	**Pakistanlı**
	p*a*h-kee-stahn-luh
Scots	**İskoçyalı**
	ees-k*o*hch-yah-luh
South African	**Guney Afrikalı**
	gooh-n*e*hy ahf-ree-kah-l*u*h
Welsh	**Galler**
	gahl-l*e*hr
West Indian	**Antilli**
	ahn-teel-l*ee*
Yugoslav	**Yugoslav**
	yoo-goh-sl*a*hv

DEPARTMENT STORE AND SHOP GUIDE

- Department stores are only just beginning to appear in Turkey, so one still has to go to a variety of shops to buy different items. This list has been compiled to help with shopping in general.

Antikacı	Antique dealer
Ayakkabıcı	Shoemaker
Ayakkabı tamircisi	Shoe repairer
Bakırcı	Coppersmith
Bakkal	Greengrocer
Balıkçı	Fishmonger
Battaniyeler	Blankets
Berber	Barber
Çantalar	Bags
Çarşaflar	Sheets
Çiçekçi	Florist
Çorap	Socks
Derici	Leather shop
Eczane	Chemist
Elbise	Clothes
Eldivenci	Gloves
Erkek kuaför	Barber

Eşarp	Scarves (for women)
Etekler	Skirts
Fotografçı	Photography shop
Fotokopi	Photocopying
Gazeteci	Newsagent
Gömlekçi	Shirtmaker
Güzellik salonu	Beauty salon
Halıcı	Carpet seller
Hatıra eşyası	Souvenirs
Havlular	Towels
Hırdavatçı	Ironmonger
Kadın çamaşırı	Lingerie
Kadın çorabı	Stockings
Kadın şapkacısı	Milliner
Kadın terzisi	Dressmaker
Kapalı çarşı	Bazaar ('covered market')
Kaşkol	Scarves (for men)
Kazaklar	Pullovers
Kemerler	Belts
Kırtasiyeci	Stationer
Kitabevi	Bookshop
Kuaför	Hairdresser
Kumaşçı	Draper
Kunduracı	Shoemaker
Kuru temizleyici	Dry cleaner
Kuyumcu	Goldsmith
Külotlu çorap	Tights
Kürkçü	Furrier
Lüleci	Pipe-maker
Manav	Greengrocer
Mandıra	Dairy
Mantolar	Women's coats
Mayolar	Bathing suits
Mobilya	Furniture
Mobilyacı	Furniture shop
Mücevherci	Jeweller
Nalbur	Hardware
Oyuncakçı	Toy shop
Paltolar	Overcoats
Pantalonlar	Trousers
Parfümöri	Parfumerie
Pastacı	Confectioner

Pastane	Cake shop
Saatçi	Watchmaker
Sarraf	Moneychanger
Seramik	Ceramics, chinaware
Seyahat acentası	Travel agent
Spor mağazası	Sports shop
Sütçü	Milkman
Şapkacı	Hatter
Şarapçı	Wine merchant
Şarap tüccarı	Wine merchant
Şarkütöri	Delicatessen
Şekerci	Confectioner
Şekerleme	Confectionery
Şemsiyeler	Umbrellas
Tatlıcı	Pastry shop
Terlik	Slippers
Terzi	Tailor
Turizm acentası	Travel agent
Tuhafiyeci	Haberdashery
Tütüncü	Tobacconist
Zücaciyeci	Glassware

CONVERSION TABLES

Read the centre column of these tables from right to left to convert from metric to imperial and from left to right to convert from imperial to metric e.g. 5 litres = 8.80 pints; 5 pints = 2.84 litres

pints		litres		gallons		litres
1.76	1	0.57		0.22	1	4.55
3.52	2	1.14		0.44	2	9.09
5.28	3	1.70		0.66	3	13.64
7.07	4	2.27		0.88	4	18.18
8.80	5	2.84		1.00	5	22.73
10.56	6	3.41		1.32	6	27.28
12.32	7	3.98		1.54	7	31.82
14.08	8	4.55		1.76	8	36.37
15.84	9	5.11		1.98	9	40.91

ounces		grams
0.04	1	28.35
0.07	2	56.70
0.11	3	85.05
0.14	4	113.40
0.18	5	141.75
0.21	6	170.10
0.25	7	198.45
0.28	8	226.80
0.32	9	255.15

pounds		kilos
2.20	1	0.45
4.41	2	0.91
6.61	3	1.36
8.82	4	1.81
11.02	5	2.27
13.23	6	2.72
15.43	7	3.18
17.64	8	3.63
19.84	9	4.08

inches		centimetres
0.39	1	2.54
0.79	2	5.08
1.18	3	7.62
1.58	4	10.16
1.95	5	12.70
2.36	6	15.24
2.76	7	17.78
3.15	8	20.32
3.54	9	22.86

yards		metres
1.09	1	0.91
2.19	2	1.83
3.28	3	2.74
4.37	4	3.66
5.47	5	4.57
6.56	6	5.49
7.66	7	6.40
8.65	8	7.32
9.84	9	8.23

miles		kilometres
0.62	1	1.61
1.24	2	3.22
1.86	3	4.83
2.49	4	6.44
3.11	5	8.05
3.73	6	9.66
4.35	7	11.27
4.97	8	12.87
5.59	9	14.48

A quick way to convert kilometres to miles: divide by 8 and multiply by 5. To convert miles to kilometres: divide by 5 and multiply by 8.

fahrenheit (°F)	centigrade (°C)		lbs/ sq in	k/ sq cm
212°	100°	boiling point	18	1.3
100°	38°		20	1.4
98.4°	36.9°	body temperature	22	1.5
86°	30°		25	1.7
77°	25°		29	2.0
68°	20°		32	2.3
59°	15°		35	2.5
50°	10°		36	2.5
41°	5°		39	2.7
32°	0°	freezing point	40	2.8
14°	−10°		43	3.0
−4°	−20°		45	3.2
			46	3.2
			50	3.5
			60	4.2

To convert °C to °F: divide by 5, multiply by 9 and add 32. To convert °F to °C: take away 32, divide by 9 and multiply by 5.

CLOTHING SIZES

Remember – always try on clothes before buying. Clothing sizes are usually unreliable.

women's dresses and suits

Europe	38	40	42	44	46	48
UK	32	34	36	38	40	42
USA	10	12	14	16	18	20

men's suits and coats

Europe	46	48	50	52	54	56
UK and USA	36	38	40	42	44	46

men's shirts

Europe	36	37	38	39	41	42	43
UK and USA	14	14½	15	15½	16	16½	17

socks

Europe	38–39	39–40	40–41	41–42	42–43
UK and USA	9½	10	10½	11	11½

shoes

Europe	34	35½	36½	38	39	41	42	43	44	45
UK	2	3	4	5	6	7	8	9	10	11
USA	3½	4½	5½	6½	7½	8½	9½	10½	11½	12½

Do it yourself

Some notes on the language

This section does not deal with 'grammar' as such. The purpose here is to explain some of the most obvious and elementary nuts and bolts of the language, based on the principal phrases included in the book. This information should enable you to produce numerous sentences of your own making.

There is no pronunciation in this section, partly because it would get in the way of the explanations and partly because you have to do it yourself at this stage if you are serious – work out the pronunciation from all the earlier examples in the book.

NOUNS

- **Singular:** the word for a/an in Turkish is **bir** ('one'). However, when referring to a noun in general, the noun is used without an article of any kind. Similarly, the noun on its own can also mean some/any.
- **Plural:** the plural is formed by adding **-ler/-lar** to the end of the noun.

	Singular		Plural
an address	**adres**	addresses	**adresler**
an apple	**elma**	apples	**elmalar**
a beer	**bira**	beers	**biralar**
a bill	**hesap**	bills	**hesaplar**
a bus	**otobüs**	buses	**otobüsler**
a (cup of) tea	**çay**	teas	**çaylar**
a key	**anahtar**	keys	**anahtarlar**
a menu	**mönü**	menus	**mönüler**
a newspaper	**gazete**	newspapers	**gazeteler**
a receipt	**makbuz**	receipts	**makbuzler**
a restaurant	**lokanta**	restaurants	**lokantalar**
a roll	**sandviç**	rolls	**sandviçler**
a room	**oda**	rooms	**odalar**
a telephone	**telefon**	telephones	**telefonlar**
a timetable	**tarife**	timetables	**tarifeler**

- When adding **-ler/-lar** to make the noun plural, how do you choose which ending to use? This depends on the last vowel of the noun. If it is: e, i, ö, ü add **ler**
  a, ı, o, u **lar**
  This is called the principle of vowel harmony, whereby the vowels of endings added to words (for instance, to form plurals) change to harmonize with the sound of the root word.
- Does it matter? Not unless you want to make a serious attempt to speak correctly and scratch below the surface of the language. You would generally be understood whichever of the plural endings you added to a noun. However, if you listen to what people say, you will soon pick up which is the correct one to add.

Using the words in the above table, practise saying and writing these sentences in Turkish:

Have you got a receipt?	**Makbuz var mı?**
a telephone?	**. . . var mı?**
I'd like a beer	**Bira istiyorum**
some rolls	**. . . istiyorum**
Where can I get a newspaper?	**Gazete nerede bulabilirim?**
a cup of tea?	**. . . nerede bulabilirim?**
Is there a key?	**Anahtar var mı?**
a telephone?	**. . . var mı?**
a timetable?	
a restaurant?	
a menu?	
Are there any rooms?	**Odalar var mı?**
any newspapers?	**. . . var mı?**
any keys?	

Now try to make up more sentences along these same lines using other vocabulary in the book.

THE

- There is no word for 'the' in Turkish. But if a word is the object of a sentence a vowel ending is added to the word. Once again this vowel is chosen according to the principle of vowel harmony.

- If the final vowel of the noun is: **e** or **i** add **i**

ö	ü	ü
a	ı	ı
o	u	u

- If the noun actually ends in a vowel, a **-y** is inserted as a buffer between the root word and the vowel ending.

address	**adresi**	addresses	**adresleri**
apple	**emlayı**	apples	**elmaları**
beer	**birayı**	beers	**biraları**
bill	**hesabı**	bills	**hesapları**
bus	**otobüsü**	buses	**otobüsleri**
cup of tea	**çayı**	cups of tea	**çayları**
key	**anahtarı**	keys	**anahtarları**
menu	**mönüyü**	menus	**mönüleri**
newspaper	**gazeteyi**	newspapers	**gazeteleri**
receipt	**makbuzu**	receipts	**makbuzları**
restaurant	**lokantayı**	restaurants	**lokantaları**
roll	**sandviçi**	rolls	**sandviçleri**
room	**odayı**	rooms	**odaları**
telephone	**telefonu**	telephones	**telefonları**
timetable	**tarifeyi**	timetables	**tarifeleri**

Using the words in the table above, practise saying and writing these sentences in Turkish:

Have you got the key?	**Anahtarı var mı?**
the timetable?	**. . . var mı?**
the address?	
the menu?	
I'd like the receipt	**Makbuzu istiyorum**
the bill	**. . . istiyorum**
the keys	
Where is the timetable?	**Tarifeyi nerede?**
the key?	**. . . nerede?**
the address?	
the restaurant?	
the room?	

Where are the rolls?	**Sandviçleri nerede?**
the keys?	**. . . nerede?**
the apples?	
the rooms?	
the buses?	
Where can I get the address?	**Adresi nerede bulabilirim?**
the key?	**. . . nerede bululabilirim?**
the	
timetables?	

VAR/YOK

- There is no word, in the English sense, for 'have' in Turkish. Instead, the words **var** (literally, 'existent') and **yok** (literally, 'non-existent') are used. To make these words into questions, **var** is followed by the word **mı**, and **yok** by the word **mu**:

Is there/are there?	**Var mı?**
Isn't there/aren't there?	**Yok mu?**

- In reply, you will hear:

Var	There is/there are
Yok	There isn't/there aren't (any)

Practise writing and saying these sentences in Turkish (remembering that to say 'some/any', just use the word on its own):

Have you got some coffee?	**Kahve var mı?**
some wine?	**. . . var mı?**
some bread?	
Is there any water?	**Su var mı?**
any cheese?	**. . . var mı?**
any tea?	
Are there any keys?	
Isn't there any beer?	**Bira yok mu?**
any water?	**. . . yok mu?**
any wine?	
Aren't there any newspapers?	

THIS/THAT

Use these three words in Turkish:

Bu this	**Şu** that (nearby)	**O**	that (further away)

If you don't know the Turkish for something you can use these words, pointing to what you want. If you use them with a verb, add **-nu** to the end of them:

Bunu istiyorum	I want this
Şunu istiyorum	I want that
Onu istiyorum	I want that (over there)
Bunu istiyorum	I need this

HELPING OTHERS

You can help yourself with phrases such as:

I'd like . . . a roll	**Sandviç . . . istiyorum**
Where can I get . . . a (cup of) tea?	**Çay . . . nerede bulabilirim?**
I need . . . a receipt	**Makbuz . . . istiyorum**
I'd like . . . a beer	**Bira . . . istiyorum**

If you come across a compatriot having trouble making himself or herself understood, you should be able to speak to the Turkish person on their behalf. (A pronunciation guide is provided from here on, to help you with the unfamiliar parts of each phrase.)

● Note that you use the same verb form for he or she in Turkish.

He'd like . . .	**Sandviç . . . istiyor** sahnd-v*ee*ch . . . ees-t*ee*-yohr
She'd like . . .	**Bira . . . istiyor** b*ee*-rah . . . ees-t*ee*-yohr
Where can he get . . .?	**Çay . . . nerede bulabilir?** chay . . . neh-reh-d*eh* boo-lah-bee-l*ee*r
Where can she get . . .?	**Sandviç . . . nerede bulabilir?** sahnd-v*ee*ch . . . neh-reh-d*eh* boo-lah-bee-l*ee*r
He'll have . . .	**Çay . . . ister** chay . . . ees-t*eh*r
She'll have . . .	**Neskafe . . . ister** nehs-kah-f*eh* . . . ees-t*eh*r
He needs . . .	**Makbuz . . . istiyor** mahk-b*ooz* . . . ees-t*ee*-yohr
She needs . . .	**Bilet . . . istiyor** bee-l*eh*t ees-t*ee*-yohr

You can also help a couple or a group if they are having difficulties.

- To make the plural 'they' form of the verb, add **-ler/-lar** to the
  he/she form, following the same rule of vowel harmony described
  above in the section on forming plural nouns.

They'd like . . .	**Peynir . . . istiyorlar**
	pehy-ne*er* . . . ees-tee-yohr-l*a*hr
Where can they get . . .?	**Aspirin . . . nerede bulabilirler?**
	ahs-pee-re*en* . . . neh-reh-d*e*h boo-
	lah-bee-leer-l*eh*r
They'll have . . .	**Şarap . . . isterler**
	shah-r*a*hp . . . ees-tehr-l*eh*r
They need . . .	**Şu . . . istiyorlar**
	shoo . . . ees-tee-yohr-l*a*r

What about the two of you? No problem. Once again you change
the verb ending.

- Taking the he/she form of the verb, if the final vowel is:
  e or i add **iz**

ö	ü	**üz**
a	ı	**ız**
o	u	**uz**

We'd like . . .	**Şarap . . . istiyoruz**
	shah-r*a*hp . . . ees-*tee*-yoh-rooz
Where can we get . . .?	**Şu . . . nerede bulabiliriz?**
	shoo . . . neh-reh-d*e*h boo-lah-bee-
	lee-reez
We'll have . . .	**Bira . . . isteriz**
	b*ee*-rah . . . ees-t*eh*-reez
We need . . .	**Aspirin . . . istiyoruz**
	ahs-pee-re*en* . . . ees-t*ee*-yoh-rooz

USEFUL WORDS

Try writing out and memorizing these six useful words:

I want/need	**İstiyorum**
	ees-*tee*-yoh-room

I don't want/need	**İstemiyorum**
	ees-*teh*-mee-yoh-room
I know	**Biliyorum**
	bee-*lee*-yoh-room
I don't know	**Bilmiyorum**
	b*eel*-mee-yoh-room
I understand	**Anlıyorum**
	ahn-*luh*-yoh-room
I don't understand	**Anlamıyorum**
	ahn-*lah*-muh-yoh-room

MORE PRACTICE

Here are some more Turkish names of things. See how many different sentences you can make up, using the various points of information given earlier in this section.

		Singular	Plural
1	ashtray	**küllük**	**küllükler**
2	bag	**çanta**	**çantalar**
3	car	**araba**	**arabalar**
4	cigarette	**sigara**	**sigaralar**
5	corkscrew	**tirbuşon**	**tirbuşonlar**
6	deckchair	**şezlong**	**şezlonglar**
7	garage (repairs)	**tamirhane**	**tamirhaneler**
8	grapes	**üzüm**	**üzümler**
9	ice-cream	**dondurma**	**dondurmalar**
10	melon	**kavun**	**kavunlar**
11	passport	**pasaport**	**pasaportlar**
12	postcard	**kartpostal**	**kartpostallar**
13	salad	**salata**	**salatalar**
14	shoe	**ayakkabı**	**ayakkabılar**
15	stamp	**pul**	**pullar**
16	station	**istasyon**	**istasyonlar**
17	suitcase	**valiz**	**valizler**
18	telephone	**telefon**	**telefonlar**
19	telephone jeton	**jeton**	**jetonlar**
20	ticket	**bilet**	**biletler**

Index